"FINISHING ON FIRE"

Live Your Legacy of Purpose Passion & Prosperity

DEDICATED TO:

JOE (ROBERT JOSEPH) WADSWORTH

WRITTEN BY
DAVE W. WADSWORTH

EDITORS:
ADAM LEE WADSWORTH
&
ARMANDO GARCIA

INTRODUCTION

ARE YOU ?? ------ YES, I'M TALKING TO YOU!!

A Happy Man? - Contented Man? - A Regret Free Man?

Imagine your life full of Purpose & Passion & Prosperity.

No worries, No time clocks, No regrets from yesterday,

No concerns for tomorrow. Living FULLY ALIVE.

YOU – *A free & majestic eagle soaring on the breeze of the moment.* ***Truly Happy - Truly Content - Truly Free***

Each Day immersed in fun, fascination & freedom.

Enjoying God's indescribable creation in ***Everyone***, ***Everything*** *and* ***Every Moment*** *you have left.*

The new Curious, Caring and Creative You. Living in, and for, the moment. ***Living FULLY ALIVE*** 😊

Yes, **YOU**, *in a magical playground of your own choosing.*

A playground that no amount of money could buy.

Enjoy unique, exciting & special experiences every day.

DAVE WADSWORTH

FINISHING ON FIRE

LIVE YOUR LEGACY OF PURPOSE
PASSION & PROSPERITY

R.I.P.

(YOUR NAME HERE)

NO REGRETS
NO RESERVATIONS
NO RETREAT

MEN PLEASE LIVE YOUR FINAL LAP IN LIFE WITH PURPOSE, PASSION & PROSPERITY

Let us RUN with perseverance the RACE marked out for us.

Hebrews 12:1

"I'M RACING TO THE END!!"

That's the cheerful answer I get when I ask my dear friend Steve Blankenberger (Age 72) how he is doing.

Steve enjoys life every day and truly inspires me to do likewise. He is talking more about living a full life each day. Not just a rushed or hurried life.

How Soon? **NOW!!** *Yes, today.*

How Much? **FREE!!** *No Joke, A bargain*

How? **CHOOSE IT!!** *Read On For the Answers.*

Today, **YOU** *can begin living your life of*

PURPOSE, **PASSION** *and* **PROSPERITY**.

THANK YOU!!

For Reading this book and making your life better. I'm honored to help you in your journey. May you take just one idea written here and multiply your happiness and life success. Thanks again and all my best to you and your family.

DAVE WADSWORTH

"FINISHING ON FIRE"

Live Your Legacy of Purpose Passion & Prosperity

DEDICATION

This book is dedicated to my second favorite man of all time, Robert Joseph "JOE" Wadsworth; aka "My Dad".

June 14, 1931 – May 19, 2016

My dad was always humming, whistling and smiling. I have to thank him for my early appreciation of optimism and relentless cheerfulness. Dad had an inquisitive mind and a huge generous heart. Thanks to dad I have always enjoyed an unquenchable thirst and deep passion for learning. Although reading was not my primary form of learning I always wanted to go, see, and do, new and exciting things.

In a strange mental growth-spurt I have made amazing and almost unbelievable changes in my learning through reading.

FACT #1:

For 55 years of my life I read no more than a grand total of 25 books (I guess I preferred to watch the movie version). No, I'm not real proud of this under-achievement. I was well below the 1 book per year average of most adults. That dismal fact makes this next fact a point approaching unbelievable. Fact #2 is actually astonishing, fascinating and bewildering to myself and others.

FACT #2:

Since my lackluster reading start (25 books in 55 Years) I have documented reading over 2,000 books in just 4 years. (Insert GULP here) + (Add a look of suspicious bewilderment.)

WHAT??

Yes, this sounds absurd to me as well. I know you are thinking my library must contain a mix of 20-minute quick read comics & coloring books. Yes, some books were fairly short. However, you should consider this ridiculous fact: These readings have included cover to cover of the entire Holy Bible 5 times in one year. Yes, Genesis through Revelation. Wow, "What's up with that?", is a question I continue to ask myself.

My titles include ***self -improvement, business, marketing, motivational, biographies, science, nature, sports stories, professional speaking, history, communication, religious/spiritual, humorous, sales, health & nutrition, technology, novels and many more.***

I came out of a dark period in mid-life that I describe as a valley that was deep, dark & soul crushing. It was like I was reborn and came alive like the first flowers of spring. I came alive with the vigor of a caged animal newly released into the wild. Since my reading speed is truly very average, I found that course of action tedious at best. Although I do read many print books I have found that Audible is my new best friend. It takes focused effort to average reading/listening-to more than one book per day.

Since I can't meet all the amazing people on earth, both living now and passed on in history, I can read their writings and the ideas and values they espoused. I can't encourage you enough to do this also.

I recently met a gentleman from Washington State on my plane ride to Denver. He quoted someone as saying "Read 1,000 books and Live 1,000 Lifetimes". What an amazing way you can live to your fullest (Finish on Fire) by experiencing the life & values of great people through reading their books.

Technology has been a tremendous ally in my learning quest since the vast majority are audio books. Some books I like are not available on audio so I read them aloud into my phone voice recorder so I can listen to them over and over.

Did I mention that my granddad Russell Wadsworth (Dads father) was known as the biggest reader, of his time, in Odon, Indiana. Granddad suffered a tragic logging accident while clearing land for building the Crane Naval Weapons Center. This accident left him severely handicapped and thus reading became a huge part of his later years.

I'm also proud to own my dad's full collection (86 books strong) of his favorite Western Writer LOUIS L'AMOUR. *I often remember watching dad read through the Bible many evenings while he sat at the kitchen table. With all that said I want to credit my favorite knowledge and wisdom seeker, my dad, with his constant encouragement and inspiration.*

My Hero, Joe *Wadsworth. I love* you, dad.

"FINISHING ON FIRE"

Live Your Legacy of Purpose
Passion & Prosperity

I BELIEVE:

Reading *is* ***Learning****,*

Learning *is* ***Growing****,*

Growing *leads to,*

Happiness *and* ***Success****.*

Dad, thanks for helping me be happy and successful. I love you.

Dad before his stroke.

Last Photo with Dad, Sarah(daughter), Doug (brother), Glenda my wife and myself.

"FINISHING ON FIRE"

Live Your Legacy of Purpose
Passion & Prosperity

REFLECTION & ACTION

Throughout this book I am going to ask you to do something very strange. You will have to buck all your school teachers, learned general rules of decent behavior and forge a new habit. At the end of many chapters I'm asking you to participate in an exercise that I know you will find challenging and rewarding. You will be asked a handful of questions regarding what you just read and then seriously consider your past, present and future responses. Yes, I am asking you to actually write in this book. Don't just think through these questions but actually write your thoughts on the pages provided. I promise you will be glad you did this. It's only a few minutes but they can be life altering minutes.

All the best to you.

"FINISHING ON FIRE"

Live Your Legacy of Purpose
Passion & Prosperity

"FINISHING ON FIRE"

Live Your Legacy of Purpose
Passion & Prosperity

TO CONTACT THE AUTHOR:

davewadsworth777@gmail.com

Phone: 812-499-5090

Website: FINISHINGonFIRE.com

ISBN – 9798654343192

Published by Dave W. Wadsworth Publishing

Printed in the United States of America

Edited by Adam Lee Wadsworth & Armando Garcia

"FINISHING ON FIRE"

Live Your Legacy of Purpose
Passion & Prosperity

TO MY FAMILY

On Holidays we meet at the home of one of my brothers. Christmas Eve is always at Kelly & Telesa's beautiful home in Odon, IN. All other holidays are at my brother Doug's house in Washington, IN. Doug, thanks for remodeling to accommodate our expanding family. My sister Myra & her family have to fly in from San Diego, California (Bring your coat).

These are always times of fun, food and fellowship. We make a large family circle and hold hands to pray and express thanks for all our blessings. I am always thankful for enjoying the best family in the whole world. Young and old and without exception the entire Wadsworth family rocks.

Live Your Legacy of Purpose
Passion & Prosperity

CONTENTS

1. HARPER LEE AT 3

What is your life? You are a mist (a fleeting vapor) that appears for a little while and then vanishes.

James 4:14

We each choose how we live our "fleeting" lives. We can live in **FEAR** *or in* **FAITH***. You don't have to be a particularly religious person to live a life of* FAITH. *An optimistic or hopeful person lives in faith every day. They look for the good in people. They look for the good in situations. They look for the good in themselves. They see a solution in every problem.*

The person living in fear always sees a problem in every solution. Their fear creates a "scarcity" mentality. The faithful person lives and promotes the "abundance" mentality. This book reveals a solid pathway for you to travel your journey with hopeful passion and abundant living.

Wonder, excitement and unbridled enthusiasm was how your life began. Play, discovery and creativity with relentless enthusiasm and happiness. You repeated this cycle every day until you dropped with exhaustion. Go, See & Do with reckless abandon. That's how I remember my fantastic early days. Sadly, now the terms Carefree, Regret Free and Time Free are all but vanquished memories of those early years of life.

Why do days seem to drag on while years fly by? You, my friend, are aboard the speeding train of life. A single snowball rolling down the mountain of life gaining speed while losing control. You have seemingly lost control of the throttle, direction and the brake. This book will provide you with 100% control of your life's throttle, direction and brake.

Good news: YOU *are the architect of your life (insert smile) + (Add a sigh of relief) + (visualize a strong glimmer of hope)*

"Architect" - *The Creator and Designer of things.*

Bad News: *You have been the architect of your life to this point (insert dismayed look here)*

HONESTY AGREEMENT TIME

YOU, *ate the cheeseburgers, pizza and pies that made you fat (I know I did)*
+ **YOU**, *chose "healthy?" exercise habits daily*
+ **YOU**, *picked your mate for life*
+ **YOU**, *selected and completed your career, education level, and/or training*
+ **YOU**, *applied for and accepted every job (and salary) you worked for*

+ **YOU**, *chose the friends you hung out with*

+ **YOU**, *chose the movies you watched*

+ **YOU**, *chose the books you would read (or not)*

+ **YOU**, ...***Get the Picture*** 😊

FOR THE OSTRICH MEN WHO DISAGREE WITH ME ON THAT LAST POINT OF BAD NEWS; THIS BOOK WILL NOT HELP YOU UNTIL THAT POINT IS HONESTLY RECONCILED IN YOUR HEAD FIRST.

I WILL JUST WAIT HERE QUIETLY FOR YOU TO GET IT.
OK, TIME'S UP.
GET IT, OR CHUCK THIS BOOK IN THE TRASH.
BETTER YET, GO ASK YOUR 5 CLOSEST AND BRUTALLY HONEST FRIENDS ABOUT MY "BAD NEWS" STATEMENT OF TRUTH! IF THEY DON'T AGREE THAT YOUR LIFE, TO THIS POINT, IS TOTALLY (99%) YOUR FAULT (YOUR CHOICES). WELL, I SUGGEST YOU DUMP THEM AND GO GET NEW, HONEST, FRIENDS. (or continue living the victim role in life, truly your choice here)

WOW, That was a face slap of honesty.

*"**The TRUTH**, is always **The TRUTH**,.....*

No matter who says it, Or Who believes it."

Dave Wadsworth

Back on the Track ☺

Do you want those fun days back?

How about true Purpose in everyday living?

How about renewed Passion in your daily life?

Abundant Prosperity as your constant companion?

Are you sick and tired of being "sick and tired"? Do you live in a routine (rut filled life) of a quiet, boring existence?

Recently, I've been inspired frequently by the passion and carefree living expressed by my three-year-old granddaughter, Harper Lee Wadsworth. She helps me refocus my over-crowded and sometimes tedious life with one of fun, freedom and wonderment.

Yesterday's regrets and tomorrow's burdens are truly absent from her mind. I'm jealous and in awe of her playful "living-in-the-moment" nature. It is truly what we all are seeking. Simply put, we seek Purpose, Passion and Prosperity in everyday living.

The grand essentials for HAPPINESS are

A. Something to Love

B. Something to Do

C. Something to Hope For.

Thomas Chalmers

THE IMPORTANCE OF HAVING A PURPOSE, IN LIFE.

Purpose: *Harper lives with Purpose and zero second-guessing herself. She sees and does life at her own pace and in the manner she enjoys. Very few boundaries cage her free spirited happiness. Life is enjoyment through expression and discovery.*

Her Purpose is to live, love, laugh and sing with everyone and everything she meets. Life for Harper consists of unbridled fun, song and magical creativity.

LIVE WITH PURPOSE OR DIE

In his book titled "Kingdoms In Conflict" the late Charles Colson wrote about Purpose and human on human cruelty. Colson tells of a WW II, Nazi concentration camp that housed a factory where hundreds of Jewish prisoners were forced into hard labor.

One day the allied forces bombed and destroyed the factory. The next morning hundreds of prisoners reported to one end of the charred remains of the factory. Expecting orders to begin rebuilding the factory, they were startled by what happened next. A large pile of sand had been placed at one end of the destroyed factory. The Nazi officer gave orders for the prisoners to shovel the sand and cart it to the other end of the demolished building.

The next day the prisoner's orders were reversed. They were forced to shovel the sand and cart it back to the other end of the factory.

The prisoners naturally scoffed to each other at the ridiculous command. They thought surely a mistake had been made. The task they were forced to obey made no sense. Day after day this senseless task was repeated. Again and again they were forced to haul the same huge pile of sand to the other end of this bombed out factory. The prisoners were truly confounded by their daily orders to repeat the same meaningless and mindless task.

Then it began to happen: An elderly prisoner began crying uncontrollably until the guards hauled him away. Another man began to scream until he was beaten into unconscious silence.

A third young prisoner, who had survived three torturous years in camp, darted away from the group. The guards shouted for him to stop as he ran toward the "electrified fence". The other prisoners cried out, but it was too late. There was a blinding flash and a terrible sizzling noise as smoke puffed from his smoldering flesh. In the days that followed, dozens of prisoners "went mad". These prisoners ran from their work, only to be shot by the guards or electrocuted by the fence. The camp commandant smugly remarked that "soon they would have no more use for the gas chambers".

The gruesome lesson is plain, Colson writes,

***"Men will cling to life with dogged resolve while working meaningfully, even if that work supports their hated captors. But,* "<u>PURPOSELESS</u>" LABOR SOON SNAPS THE MIND & THE SPIRIT"**

Later in this book I will discuss very interesting tales of my personal experiences from recent travels to the Auschwitz Nazi death camps.

Back to my Harper Lee life on Purpose. Men, I have great news for you. You can recover that same free-spirited living and sense of direct purpose with the many basic ideas and actions laid out in this book.

Passion: *Boy, does little Harper live with passion. Her words, expressions and actions are all filled with passion. Sure, she exhibits A.D.D. (Attention Deficit Doing) but only because everyone and everything is filled with wonder, excitement and the opportunities of enjoyment. Passion provides her with boatloads of energy to live the good life. Have you squelched your passion for life? Have you lost your zip and zeal that children exhibit without thought or effort?*

What is your zip, zeal and passion? Every person's life is focused to "Fill a GREED", or "Meet a NEED". (Hi Guys –get out your pen. It's time to write in your book. Really. It's ok. Be different. Make the move)

5 QUESTIONS FOR PASSION DISCOVERY

What needs do I see in the world that concern me?

If I could meet any need in the world, what would that need be?

What are the most urgent needs in my country, my community, my work, my school and my church?

What age group or type of people naturally interest me?

What are the major needs among my neighbors, my friends and my family?

Honestly answering these 5 simple questions will help you determine the unique passion God has placed in your heart.

Men, Focus on meeting the needs of people and your passion will grow strong and vibrant almost overnight.

Prosperity: *Harper is the richest person on the planet. Wouldn't we be if our outlook of everyone and everything was "Gee, how much fun can they or that be?". "Come play with me?" is her constant request. True prosperity comes from the fully engaged life we see in the eyes of a three-year-old. Everyone is a playmate. Everything is a plaything. What a fantastic outlook, perspective, Attitude!*

Harper Lee with Uncle Doug and Myself.

The following pages will guide you back into that cheerful, vibrant mindset of expression and wonderment. A solid and simple action plan will bring you back genuine days of the zip, zeal and pure enjoyment of life. I Promise. Hang with me on this.

2. RADIO SHOW TO FINISH ON FIRE

The Finishing on Fire Radio Show broadcasts weekly programs of information and inspiration to build men up. These are regular shots of encouragement and action. The show comes on a worldwide podcast that can be accessed by anyone with a smartphone or computer. The Finishing on Fire Radio Show is obviously free to any men (or women) interested. My co-host, Greg Vance, is a dear friend and mentor. With wit and wisdom, the show promotes ideas to live daily with Purpose, Passion and Prosperity.

Each week a new topic or relevant question is addressed with the intent of building men of integrity.
Men, we are all searching for a life of high-value for ourselves and our families.

Here is probably a good place to introduce my PALS "Life Success" formula. I use this while doing my motivational speeches to audiences all over the world.

"PALS" FORMULA

*My Dad modeled a tremendously positive attitude for his family & friends alike. I was blessed to inherit his "look-for-the-good" attitude. In fact, my next book is entitled "**Attitude before Underwear**". In that book I will be detailing the life-changing "Attitude" formula that I have developed.*

In January of 2016 I met my dear friend and professional speaking coach Kent Julian. He is a first rate person, family man, and speaker. The PALS formula came to me through my idea brainstorming at one of his training sessions that summer. I developed this simple formula and over dinner that evening I shared it with Kent and his wife. He shared my enthusiasm and encouraged me to develop this idea for my future speaking and training engagements.

I call it my **PALS** *formula.*

PALS *is actually my acronym for* **P + A = LS.**

My speaking, coaching & training engagements involve implementing this formula into your Business, Organization or Family. Attitude is THE critical success component every person should lock into their own minds.

Since we all have **P***roblems, and all truly desire* **L***ife* **S***uccess, then that only leaves the critical bridge between those two; It is, simply put, our* **A***ttitude.*

P + A = LS *formula and acronym is:*
P*roblems +* **A***ttitude =* **L***ife* **S***uccess.*

No matter what anyone says to you.
No matter what anyone does to you.
No matter the circumstances that surround you.

"Our Attitude is the one thing that we have 100% control of"
Dave Wadsworth

It is Our choice how we respond to life & people. Not just a quick knee-jerk reaction. Reactions tend to be hurtful, damaging and actions that we will soon live to regret. No matter how good or bad it seems, we ALWAYS have a choice of Attitude.

The critical bridge to LIFE SUCCESS is your ATTITUDE, *pure and simple.*

I strongly urge you to get and read the book titled "Man's Search for Meaning" by Viktor E. Frankl. In this book Viktor writes of personal experiences like none we could imagine in America today. Through all his physical, mental, and emotional torture he triumphs over death time and time again.

Although Viktor miraculously survived, he suffered the deaths of many friends, his young wife, his mom, his dad and his brother. The loss of his home. The loss of his early medical practice. The loss of all his possessions including his highly valued scientific writings. All of this on top of his subsequent imprisonment involving constant torture, hard labor and starvation.

One huge lesson that I learned from Viktor was in his statement that "man's last freedom is his freedom to choose his ATTITUDE *in any given situation of life". The choice of deciding "one's own way" at any point in life.*

Every day, every hour and every minute we live, is completely filled with the one thing called "CHOICES"*. We make hundreds and even thousands of choices each day. These choices come in all shapes, sizes and colors. Some are life changing but many are simple and mundane. To again quote the fabulous author, Andy Andrews, "we make choices and then over time those choices...make us".*

That is the Dave Wadsworth paraphrase but it is so very true. For example: I did not walk into McDonald's one day and eat their daily "meal deal" and gain 110 extra pounds. They actually made it easy for me. By installing a handy drive-thru window, I could then lazily stay in my air conditioned car. That made the cumulative weight gain much more rapid since I didn't burn any calories by getting out of my car and actually walking into the restaurant.

My ridiculous weight gains have not been through force feedings of large quantities of unhealthy food and drinks. Every single time, I have intentionally got in my car and drove to these restaurants. I then asked for the exact unhealthy food I wanted. Then I actually pulled out my hard earned money and paid them for it.

This series of daily unhealthy choices was fully under my control. It all began with my choices. I must boldly say that all of those choices began with my Attitude. If we all look close enough we can see that everything that we have become, is and was, based on our Attitude.

3. WORLD'S BIGGEST RACE

And...........He's.............On IT!!

These words created a roar from the crowd that rattled your bones. Energy, Excitement and Anticipation shot through the gathering at breakneck speed. And speed was what today was all about.

I was only 10 years old and my $3-dollar ticket earned me a seat to witness one of the greatest engineering marvels in the world. Being from a family of very limited means we were blessed to be living a mere 100 miles away. Yes, a short three-hour drive to the World's Largest Single Day Sporting Event of the Year. The Indianapolis 500 Track is located in Speedway, Indiana just west of downtown Indianapolis.

I can still feel the early morning chill of that crisp May Saturday in Indiana. I still clearly hear the sounds of the speedway announcer's voice and excitement as it crackled over the old grandstand speakers. The unforgettable smell of popcorn, cotton candy and hotdogs, from the track-side vendors, is still strong in my nostrils. The brilliant colors of the magnificently engineered race cars are etched into my minds-eye.

The crowd was larger than nearly any other sporting event in the world. And, Guess What? This wasn't even the Official Indy 500 Race Day. It was just the first day of qualifications to see which 33 cars and drivers would make the Annual Memorial Day Race.

These marvelous race cars were painted with amazing neon colors of Orange, Red, Yellow, Green and Blue. When they zipped by at over 200 miles per hour they were just a gorgeous flash like a brilliant rainbow.

The engines roared so loud that, my brother Doug and I, always brought Kleenex tissues to stuff in our ears. Without the small wads of tissue, I think our ears and heads would have exploded.

My dad would attend the Indy 500 Qualifications (Time Trials we called them) every year without fail. It was quite a treat for men and boys alike. The day would begin with a few hours of practice runs. That's when all cars were allowed to run laps and fine tune their machines prior to their official qualification attempt. This was so exciting since you would have dozens of highly engineered world class race cars flying around the track at once.

Qualifications involved a 4 lap solo run by each car and driver. When practice runs were over, the drivers would then make their qualification attempt. Each qualifying attempt was based on a blind drawing for running order.

The car and driver would get a warmup lap or two to get up to speed and see if his car was ready to give it a go. Once this warmup was complete, the driver would signal as he approached the starting line "Yard of Bricks" to make his official qualifying run. That's when you would hear the track announcer with those famous thundering words......... **And...... He's.........On IT!!**

That's when the crowd came to life and roared louder than the racecar's engine. The car and driver now had 4 laps to run at the highest speed he could reach. The four lap speed average was then used to rank the critical race-day starting position of each car.

With each completed qualifying lap, the track announcer would boom out the lap time and the average lap speed. With each lap, the crowd's energy, excitement and anticipation would audibly, and physically build.

The tension in the air was so heavy you could actually feel it's physical presence. I promise you, it was pants-wetting excitement for a little boy of 10. Sensory overload like you can't imagine.

The track announcer was fantastic. His words and voice really added to the excitement of the moment. By the time the 4th and final lap came around the tension, excitement, and anticipation was as thick as cold honey in a jar. For a little boy, the tension, of the moment, made each lap seem like it lasted an hour. In reality the whole qualifying run was a mere 4 minutes.

Looking back on those power-filled moments I'm reminded of the vital importance of Finishing on Fire. I'm reminded how that 4th and Final Lap was so very critical. It would make or break the success of the entire qualification run.

That 4th and Final Lap was the..................

***Time to* LET IT ALL HANG OUT.**

***Time to* HOLD NOTHING BACK**

***Time to* LAY IT ALL ON THE LINE.**

***Time to* LEAVE IT ALL.....ON THE TRACK.**

MEN, THIS IS YOUR 4TH AND FINAL LAP

No Regrets

No Reservations

No Retreat

***Please hear me,* MEN, THIS IS YOUR**

4TH *and* FINAL LAP *in* LIFE

MEN…IT'S YOUR TIME

To *Live*, LETTING IT ALL HANG OUT

To *Live*, LAYING IT ALL ON THE LINE

To *Live*, HOLDING NOTHING BACK

To *Live*, LEAVING IT ALL ON THE TRACK

IT'S.................... YOUR........................ TIME.......

To *Live*....... WHO YOU ARE

To *Live*......... BEING "ALL YOU CAN BE"

To *Live*.... BEING WHO YOU WERE MEANT TO BE

To *Live*......................*the* NO REGRETS LIFE

To *Live*...................... *the* NO EXCUSES LIFE

To *Live*...............*the* PURPOSE FILLED LIFE

To *Live*...............*the* PASSION FILLED LIFE

To *Live*.........*the* PROSPERITY FILLED LIFE

MEN ....IT'S TIME – CHOOSE IT & DO IT!!

YOUR 4TH AND FINAL LAP IN LIFE

Fine Tuning for Victory

Relationship I Must Focus on: ____________

First 3 steps?

A. ____________

B. ____________

C. ____________

Health Issue I Must Focus on: ____________

First 3 steps?

A. ____________

B. ____________

C. ____________

Money Issue I Must Focus on: ____________

First 3 steps?

A. ____________

B. ____________

C. ____________

MEN, just take a minute and fill in the blanks.

OK, don't whine if you keep getting the same results.

YES, *write in the book.* NOW!!

4. 1,891 IS LARGER THAN 18.5

Not being a mathematics all-star, like my nephew, I pulled out my trusty calculator for help with this chapter. With the punching of a few buttons I quickly arrived at the answer I was looking for. Yes, 1,891 is more than 100 times larger than 18.5. Actually, with just a quick glance, I was sure they were at least 100 times apart. Hey, I did salvage a "C" in Calculus at Purdue University back in the day. No Professor bribery or cheating of any kind was involved. Although I won't rule out divine intervention working in my favor. Even my brilliant young Asian professor was shocked and amazed.
(I'll tell you the whole funny story sometime)

Driving since age 16, I've operated dozens of vehicles from motorcycles to cars to trucks and buses. I've logged well over a million miles (with no speeding tickets to date).

(Oh, that was just the kiss of death) I probably should not have stated that out loud. I can see a ticket coming in my near future - LOL. Actually I'm a pretty responsible driver overall.

My point is this: I have never, ever operated a motor vehicle without a rearview mirror. (Ok, except for my riding lawn mower.) For safety sake I don't recommend you do it either. There is a very good reason these dozens of vehicles all had that particular piece of safety equipment. Although you don't want to spend but a fraction of your driving time looking in the rearview mirror, it is extremely vital to glance at it regularly.

I like the attitude of John Lee Dumas when he states that "You either win, or you Learn". Don't let yourself be continually cast as a "Loser" in life's events. Not by others but especially not by yourself. Your (honest) opinion of you is far more important than other peoples' opinions of you. No one knows you as well as you do.

We all make mistakes and miss-steps on a regular basis. If you are a person of basically good intentions and good actions, don't keep beating yourself up. For clarity sake, if you are an obnoxious jerk and people tell you so, I would suggest that you listen and change your repulsive behavior immediately.

The following is a quote I used to tell my former students on a regular basis:

"You must learn from "other" peoples' mistakes, because you will never live long enough to make them all yourself" Dave Wadsworth

The magnificent President Abraham Lincoln was quoted as saying..... ***"I can learn something from nearly every person I meet.............However, it is usually what NOT to do"***

Regrets *are the issue at hand. Yes, 1,891 is more than 100 times as large as 18.5. Those two numbers represent the total square inch measurements of my windshield and my rearview mirror. This is on my very large pickup truck. Your vehicle will probably have similar representative measurements too.*

Regrets are something we all have behind us if we are totally honest with ourselves. Jim Rohn used to say that "the weight of discipline is very light compared to the extreme heaviness of regrets" (Dave Wadsworth paraphrase).

A huge part of Finishing on Fire is to stop looking in the rearview mirror at your past regrets.

Dave Wadsworth

Remember that our front windshield of life is more than 100 times larger than that tiny rearview mirror looking back at our past. STOP IT!! STOP IT, NOW!!

Driving through life constantly looking through our rearview mirror is a recipe for total frustration and disaster. You can't safely drive your car that way, and you certainly can't safely drive your life that way either.
STOP IT!! STOP IT, NOW!!

I have profoundly benefited from reading (or listening to) thousands of books. (MY WIFE GLENDA SAYS *(in a snarky tone) "Dave, you're not really reading all those books"* I SAY *"Technically no, but someone is reading them, so I think that* counts 😊"). *I also enjoy listening to many hours of great* Podcasts, *which yield a wealth of great ideas and quotes. Here is a great quote I heard years ago and I hope you will take it to heart.*

Yesterday is History

Tomorrow is A Mystery

Today is A GIFT

That is why they call it "THE PRESENT"

Here is my point in all of this:

Focus On *and* Enjoy *your* Life *Today* –
Focus On & Enjoy *the* People *right in front of you.*
Focus On & Enjoy *the* Actions *you are doing right now.*

I *promise you*, *that this small adjustment will revolutionize your relationships, your happiness and your overall success in life* – **IMMEDIATELY!!**

IF YOU JUST GET AND IMPLEMENT THAT LAST CONCEPT IT WILL FLAT OUT, HANDS DOWN, 100% GUARANTEED, ROCK YOUR WORLD !!!!

As *my dear friend* Ray *Edwards* says:
Get It? (*you say*) Got It! (*he says*) GOOD!

Now, stop driving your life looking through the Rearview mirror of past mistakes and regrets.

Drive Today, and each day, looking through your clear clean Windshield of Faith, Hope and Love.

Live today with Purpose, Passion and Prosperity

5. EVA FINISHED ON FIRE AUSCHWITZ # A-7063

McDonald's, that great institution of American Capitalism is the Cheeseburger King-of-the-World. I can attest to that first hand since one of their newest restaurants was located merely a mile away. EVA loved their chicken nuggets. They were her all-time favorite food. She had just "tweeted" to the world how she would have loved to have eaten them here about 75 years ago.

It was July 3, and one of the most beautiful days I can remember in all my years. Fabulous crystal blue skies with a slight scattering of puffy clouds to paint the sky. A light and varied breeze rushed through and then receded. Amazing temperatures that were unusually pleasant and not too hot for July, or any time really.

I was walking toward the world famous "Arched" gateway of Auschwitz-Birkenau. Many publications involving the Holocaust will include the gateway. That's when I suddenly noticed a circled gathering of young teenage boys. They were all dressed in distinct black t-shirts. Obviously a formal group of some kind.

I had witnessed this scene many times before and quickly surmised it was the gathering around a person of great interest, a celebrity, a star if you will. This time it was different though. Once I drew closer I could hear lovely singing from the boys to this "celebrity", "Star". They were circled around and sweetly serenading this person in song. Actually it turned out to be 3 songs, including the "Celebrity's" favorite about Impossible Dreams. Their voices were amazing and harmonized in a way that I can only describe as "Angelic". Honestly, those were my exact thoughts.

Like a bolt of lightning it hit me. Suddenly, I could now clearly see that this encircled "Celebrity" was Eva (Mozes) Kor. What, yes, it was Eva. My special friend Eva from Terre Haute, Indiana. I soon found out that the serenading group was the Teenage Boys Choir from Los Angeles, California. Chills filled my body as I realized that I was witnessing a sacred and quite special spontaneous event in world history. A beautiful boys choir from the "City of Angels" being at this exact gate, in this exact part of the world, at this exact moment in time: No, this is not simply a mere coincidence. It was a divinely orchestrated event from God, if I may boldly state.

After several minutes of hugs, kisses, pictures and autographs the "Angelic" Choir of Boys dispersed to continue their historic tour. They had traveled from Los Angeles, California around the world to Eastern Europe to engage in the most important performance of their lifetime. These sweet hearted boys were certainly too young to fully appreciate their magical encounter with EVA and the magnitude of their impromptu performance with a true "Rock Star" of humanity.

Still reeling from the serene event, I just witnessed, our small group moved only a few yards away to experience another astounding activity. We were all huddled around EVA in the arched gateway to that world-famous camp of unspeakable tortures, slavery, barbarism and massacre of innocents.

We were gathered in the very gateway to the German Nazi Death Camp known as Auschwitz – Birkenau. I stood where over 1 million innocent men, women and children entered this Nazi Concentration Camp only to be tortured, starved, worked to death or just straight out murdered. Most of those innocent victims were immediately stripped of their remaining worldly possessions and their naked lives were murdered within a few hours of arrival to Auschwitz. After spending several days touring the vast 500-acre death-camp I still can't wrap my head around the sheer evil of the whole thing.

EVA *was a bit frail and still recovering from her heart surgery, in* Indianapolis, *just that previous* February. *She was coughing from time to time as a lingering upper respiratory infection seemed to still nag her a bit. Her overall demeanor was quite cheerful. Her staff from the* CANDLES Holocaust Museum *in* Terre Haute, *that she founded, instructed us to treat her gingerly.* We *were instructed not to give* EVA *hugs but a kindly smile, positive words and the occasional fist-bump was welcomed.*

This lovely afternoon, EVA *would ride in a very nice, large, fully covered golf cart we called her* "Pope-Mobile". *At each stop around* Auschwitz *she would get out and walk with her push-cart and then sit down on it to engage our group. She told many stories and would gladly answer our many questions.*

At this moment we were fresh off the "Angelic" spontaneous serenading by the Los Angeles Teenage Boys Choir and standing in the Auschwitz gateway arch. EVA is sitting comfortably in her walker seat wearing her favorite striking blue outfit. She is giving us a pre-tour lecture about the overall history of her time spent as a prisoner here with twin sister Miriam.

The gate was several yards wide but it was tiny compared to the massive wide open death camp. As EVA spoke, the breeze would become quite brisk as it was squeezed through that gateway. I vividly remember a couple of times how that brisk breeze brought particles of dust and sand swirling around and engulfed us as EVA was speaking. At those strange moments I felt as if the souls of those million murdered innocents were wrapping EVA in a full-body hug of brother and sisterhood. They rushed around and through us to reach EVA. It was almost like they were welcoming her home in some surreal way.

It's hard to explain but it was a very spiritual and I guess holistic sensory event like no other in my life. I felt fully surrounded by life, death, and something in-between all at the same time. It felt strange but welcoming and very peaceful. I must say it was very strong and unmistakably very real. I could feel it with every fiber and sensory connection of my body, mind and spirit.

Wow, that was another unique and unexplainable event surrounding EVA that gorgeous July afternoon.

Our group then moved ahead inside the camp approximately 200 to 300 yards. This is where we stopped at the famous "Selection Platform". This is where only one solitary wooden cattle train car remained. These small "cattle cars" were meant to haul 8 or 9 head of cattle. Instead the Nazi soldiers squeezed in as many as 100 men, women and children. EVA stated that her family was forced into the cattle train car. Locked in the train car they traveled 4 days and nights with no food, water or bathroom facilities.

How the Nazis transported these families was vicious torture in and of itself.

The selection platform was the place where families were literally torn apart. Instant decisions of life and death were made by ruthless Nazi Soldiers as the train cars were unloaded. This is where EVA and twin sister Miriam were torn from their family. As best we know, their mother, father and two older sisters were immediately stripped naked and most likely murdered in the gas chamber. Their bodies were then burned in the on-site crematoriums. This was unimaginable evil we can't truly put into words or begin to fathom in our civilized minds.

Our small group was setting in a beautiful semi-circle on the selection platform. We were facing EVA and the lone cattle car awaiting to hear more of her story. EVA pulled out papers that contained letters she wrote to her mother and her father. They contained heart-wrenching details of past memories and many dreams lost.

As EVA concluded her reading she focused on a young lady sitting a few feet away who was very shaken and crying about what she just witnessed. EVA candidly asked her "why are you crying?" The lady stated that "it broke her heart and was very sad". EVA, always the biggest hearted person in the room, looked at her with beautiful, sympathetic eyes and said "don't cry honey, it turned out ok". Wow, what does it take to muster that kind of love, forgiveness and positive attitude. Especially sitting at the very place of the horrific and savage murder of all but one of your family members. Not to mention the other million plus innocents who lost their lives there too.

Ok, that was a 3rd amazing and heart shaking event I had just witnessed that afternoon. These are truly some amazing happenings for EVA, myself and our small group.

We now headed deeper into the camp to our next memorable site. We walked another several hundred yards to a beautiful grove of very large cottonwood trees.

Again our group took a seat but this time it was on a grassy area under the shade of these large and lovely trees. EVA then walked over and sat on her walker-cart to again address our group with stories and answers to more questions.

Just a few yards behind EVA was a large concrete raised monument with plaques of many languages of the world. This is where the memorial for remembering the lost souls of Auschwitz is located. It is where our group would come the next morning to light candles and express words of love and memories of family and friends of this scourge called the holocaust. I never realized someone in our group would not be with us in less than 24 hours. This spot is where I announced my sorrow for the loss of my dad's brother (my uncle) Rex Mumaw from Indiana. Rex died fighting for the United States Army in WW II. He died in the efforts to free the world of the horrible German Nazi flood of evil. I'm proud that my family was willing to shed their blood for the effort to free the innocents.

Under those large cottonwoods it was soothing and very peaceful. As EVA *spoke our attention was directed to our left. A half destroyed brick and concrete structure was less than* 50 *paces away. This was the very distinguishable remains of a large gas chamber that the* Nazis *designed, built and operated. The gas chamber was used for the sole purpose of mass murder. It was purely a death factory the* Germans *tried to destroy. It was in their hasty retreat that they attempted to hide the evidence of their wicked ways.*

Magical & mystical event #4 *occurred there in that gathering under the cottonwoods. Another camp visitor "just happened" to come by and a group member gave them a small bookmark describing our group. Of course our group represented the* CANDLES *museum created by* EVA.

We *were all amazed to learn that* EVA *and this person were connected through the camp. This mysterious visitor had a parent who was a fellow member of the* Dr. Death (Josef Mengele) *evil experiments on twins group. It was a very joyous and inspiring impromptu reunion of sorts.*

Again another miraculous turn of events that afternoon. One after the other these mystical and magical happenings just materialized before our eyes.

Moments later I walked along side EVA's *sweet ride as we cheerfully talked and enjoyed the afternoon weather.* We *were headed back toward the site of her housing barracks. This was located near the front entrance gateway to the camp.* EVA's *particular barracks at* Auschwitz-Birkenau *was long gone but the foundation was clearly in its' original location and condition.* Neighboring *barracks of the same size stood nearby and allowed us to fully appreciate what her lodging was like during her imprisonment.*

EVA *was setting comfortably and cheerfully in her walker-chair beside the granite marker at the entrance to her former* Auschwitz *barracks.* She *was in good spirits and smiling as she answered questions and took pictures with every member of our group.* What *a special time for all of us.*

She had just talked about the heinous treatment and experiments conducted on twins at the direction of Dr. Death, Dr. Josef Mengele. Her survival of those wicked experiments was nothing short of miraculous. I will have to save that amazing story for later.

Right now I was enjoying my interaction with our group and EVA. I volunteered to take dozens of pictures as group members handed me their cell phones. One after the other each excitedly posed with EVA. It was really an enjoyable experience on such a special and beautiful afternoon. EVA was truly loving it. EVA and I joked back and forth as the picture taking extravaganza went on for quite a while. She truly was a Rock Star to humanity. She made everyone feel special. A few hours later we all gathered for a delicious supper back at our hotel in Krakow, Poland. I again was blessed to spend time with EVA as we ate close to each other at the same table. EVA was at the head of the table by her son Alex. Alex is my age and we hit it off immediately when we dined together earlier in the week.

We quickly discovered our connection as fellow Purdue University Grads. "Boiler Up". Of course Alex didn't appreciate the fact that I was still a huge Indiana University Hoosier sports fan. We still have great fun with that weird combination.

Iced drinks in Europe are a fairly rare commodity. I'm purely All-American and that means I love my iced drinks. I especially enjoy my all-time favorite small crunchy ice. This is available at any Sonic Drive-In where a half priced Rte. 44 Coke with Extra Ice is the order of the day. In Europe however, ice free drinks are the standard. You typically get funny looks, from the servers, when you ask for an iced drink and then an extra glass of ice on the side.

Tonight's ice-free meal was no exception. Ice did however play a part in a funny exchange with EVA, myself and everyone at our table. The usual water (iceless) was served to everyone at our table.

Tonight we had these nice crystal glasses that curved in at the top. The server soon brought out my ice in a separate glass and the fun quickly began. As I tried to gracefully pour the ice into my crystal glass, of water, two ice cubes wedged on top and refused to go in. They were frozen together like attached twins. This frozen chunk created a little ice-bridge that perched on top of my glass.

The group had gotten to know the real playful Dave Wadsworth by now and wasn't surprised by the following events. I reached out to touch and possibly dislodge the crazy ice cube bridge on top of my glass. To my surprise just a finger nudge and the two cubes began spinning around the rim of that crystal glass like a toy top. It was actually quite fascinating.

Across the table Chad and Megan were quick to be amused by this spinning ice. Of course the second and third nudging attempts resulted in much more spinning acrobatics by those silly ice cubes. Just then, Alex Kor began to laugh and point.

He quickly said to EVA, "hey mom, check out Dave and his ice cube circus". By then everyone at the table was laughing and quite amused at the ice cube wedgie and the spinning spectacle. Finally, EVA looks right at me and asks "Are you a comedian?". I just laughed and told her that I do tend to make people laugh. I do really have a knack for lifting their spirits. The whole table really enjoyed my show of the "Ice Capades" and the evening dining experience was such fun.

EVA, only minutes later finished her desert, and feeling a bit tired, she excused herself to go up to her room to bed.

Just a few hours later, my friend, EVA (Mozes) Kor was gone. She died in her room.

She was truly a "Fire Cracker" so it is fitting that it was July 4th.

The news shocked the world and traveled everywhere instantly as she had touched so very many. Her message of forgiveness was Genuine and Life Changing for countless thousands.

At 85 years old, standing 5 ft. 4 inches tall she was 100 lbs. soaking wet. She was fierce, friendly and SPUNKY. A true "Fire Cracker" of a lady. Not a single 300 lb. NFL lineman would have the grit or stamina to beat her, on the battlefield of life. She lived with a full heart and was focused on FORGIVENESS like a laser.

Interesting aside ---- *Remember my description of the Indy 500 being the largest 1-day Sporting Event in the World. Well, just a few years earlier EVA was proudly serving as the Grand Marshall for that event. Big Deal. Huge Deal. Well, you, music lovers may enjoy this little tidbit of trivia. The day EVA passed I was talking with and trying to console her son Alex.*

He said "hey Dave, I got an interesting call a while ago". I said please tell me about it. Alex said that his cell phone rang a bit earlier and he saw it was someone from Los Angeles "City of Angels". He said that seemed interesting so he answered it. It was none-other than famous hard rock star Nikki Sixx, the founder of Motley Crue. He was so kind and told Alex how sorry he was about EVA's loss and how much she had helped him through his forgiveness issues. He just heard the news of EVA's death about the time they experienced an earthquake there in LA. He said to himself about the earthquake "Yep, there goes EVA". Sure thing. 4th of July. EVA the Fire Cracker. Sure makes sense to me.

Back to the Indy 500 thing. While serving as Grand Marshall and enjoying the various activities involved with that amazing event, countless numbers of celebrities meet and mingle throughout the weekend. During one such event, long haired, tattooed, rock star (Nikki Sixx) meets 83 year old holocaust survivor.

Instantly a blossoming friendship begins. There were no barriers with EVA. She lived and preached Forgiveness and Hope like no other could.

EVA is my greatest personal example of "Finishing on Fire". She lived every day to the max. I should know. I was blessed to spend that last one with her. It was truly special.

Dave Wadsworth

Footnote: CANDLES stands for Children of Auschwitz Nazi Deadly Lab Experiments Survivors.

With Eva Kor in Auschwitz at her barracks a few hours before our last supper together.

MEN Let's Do It. Finish Your Life On Fire!

6. "MARGIN" IT'S NOT ABOUT SPEED - IT'S ABOUT ACCURACY

Live Smarter, Not Harder

Dave Wadsworth

My wife has certainly earned her Angel Wings and Halo after 35 years of marriage to me. Lots of bumps, bruises and bad times. Many, many more moments of love, happiness and true contentment. Caring, communication and serious commitment are critical to build a marriage of nearly 4 decades. It all comes down to Faith, Hope and Love as stated in "The Good Book". 35 Years has certainly not been easy but it has sure been an adventure. (all men nod and insert smile here – but not while your wife is looking......LOL)

Steve, my friend, says he is "RACING to the end" as a cheerful response when asked how he is doing. What Steve is really saying is **"HIS LIFE IS PACKED FULL *of*.......LIFE"**. *Steve understands that it's not about How Fast He Is Speeding Through Life.*

Life is not about how fast we are speeding through it........ It's the Fullness of the Life we are Living as it Speeds by.
Dave Wadsworth

Bob Proctor talks about the key being "Awareness". We are all seeking a greater level of awareness. Awareness in our relationships is the most fulfilling. Awareness in our Purpose and the Passions we pursue. Awareness of the People we are sharing this very moment with. Awareness of the enjoyment opportunities in this moment. Awareness of this fact in each and every moment. Slow your speed of life down and open your eyes to the magnificence of the moment. Awareness leads to living your best life.

New quarterbacks in the National Football League always talk about the speed of the game. They say the game is played at such a faster speed than they have ever experienced it before. The key for them is awareness. They are constantly working to see the game at a slower speed so they can react and play within the flow of the new level.

Ok Men, time for some more bumps and bruises. If I'm lucky my wife won't read this chapter. I know you're saying "good luck with that one buddy boy". Here goes. My wife and I own several acres of property and I built a nice lake with 2 islands and some fun things like a Zip Line and a huge Rope Swing. Some people refer to our place as "Wadsy World".

Part of owning several acres means the necessity of owning a very large riding lawn mower. We love our large Zero-Turn mower and it does a fantastic job.

I actually told the mower salesmen, at the time of purchase, that I was looking for something rugged enough that my wife couldn't tear it up. I know you guys are agreeing and laughing about that one. I'm really getting a smack-down for this whole story but it serves as a fantastic illustration of my point.

"It's NOT *about* Speed.......It's About *Accuracy*"

Dave Wadsworth

It seems like I've told my wife that a million times. Slow down and be safe (and don't tear anything up). You can drive full speed on the straight-aways but please slow down on the turns and especially the sharp turns around objects. I honestly think she is playing "bumper cars" when she is mowing. Bouncing and banging on trees, landscaping rocks or anything that dares to stay on our property while she is riding the mower.

Pioneer days in Indiana (like when Abe Lincoln used to live just a few miles away from here) meant clearing land for farming by girdling trees to kill them. They cut a ring around the lower part of a tree that just basically peeled the bark off. This would quickly kill the trees. I have accused my wife of taking up that girdling practice using the mower on our trees.

When we first got our big mower she was not used to the large safety roll-bar it had on the back. Her early mowing experience created a very funny but dangerous event. While mowing near the lake the roll-bar caught on a safety guide wire I used to secure the large poles to our rope swing. As she went under the safety wire it caught the roll bar and caused the mower front end to pop a wheelie. Luckily she didn't flip the mower completely over backwards. In a state-of-panic she just stopped and shut the mower off right there. When she ran to me for help I found the mower standing up on its' rear wheels like some kind of redneck stunt show act. Yes, front wheels up in the air at about a 45 degree angle. (Should have taken a picture of that one 😊.)

MEN, *it's about margin in our lives*. *Room to breathe. Room to pursue and run at the pace of our individual peak performance. Running or racing through life has to be done at our optimum speed. Some of us are jack rabbits that operate best with short bursts of flashing speed. Some of us are turtles that function best just plodding along at a steady even pace. Find the ideal speed at which you can fully experience life. The speed at which you can fully appreciate people and places and things. Fully living with and through the moments. Fully living within each day. Not looking ahead too far or constantly lost in yesterday.*

The gift of life is right in front of you.

***The gift of life is today.* The "PRESENT".**

KEY QUOTE: My Gift to You

Your PRESENT (*gift*)

Is to

Be PRESENT.....

***In the* PRESENT**

7. FLAGS OF LIFE

Flags of Life are all around us and guide our basic movement. Every race track, in the world, uses a combination of specifically colored flags that control the racing event. In our everyday life we have traffic signs and signals that control our movement. These allow for the safety of ourselves, other drivers and pedestrians as well. In a civilized society these generally accepted measures are critical for orderly movement and the general wellbeing of everyone.

I would like to describe and define, the use of, the various flags commonly used on race tracks throughout the world. Men, I would also like to discuss them briefly as it relates to the living of our lives on a regular basis.

GREEN FLAG: **START** *of the race or a* **RESTART**

YELLOW FLAG: **HAZARDOUS** *situation, slow down*

RED FLAG: **DANGER**, *the race stops immediately*

BLACK FLAG: **STOP NOW** *and return to Pit area*

WHITE FLAG: **FINAL LAP** *of your race*

CHECKERED FLAG: **FINISHED** *your race*

MEN, I *bring you fantastic news*. *If you are reading this book there is still time for you. YES, you are still in this great race we call life. The question for you is; Just where are you at in that race of life? Which color flag is the signal directing your life right now? It's not the famous Black & White Checkered flag since you are not quite finished with your race yet. Let's take a look and determine your status.*

GREEN FLAG: *Your first green flag was many years ago at the "Start" (birth) of your life. Tremendous joy surrounded that event. People laughed while you cried. Here is a tremendous quote from a favorite author of mine.*

"When you were born, people rejoiced and laughed while you cried. Now, Live your Life so that when you die, You will laugh and rejoice while others Cry"

Robin Sharma

Your first Green Flag flashed at your birth and you weren't able to recognize it.

I have more good news. The Green Flag not only signals "The Start" of your race, it has a second function. That second function is your race **"Restart"**. *Wow, that means you get another chance to begin again. The opportunity in life to begin again is the most exhilarating and freeing feeling of hope that we have.*

Men, you have the Green Flag to begin again. Today. Right now. Don't put it off. I'm begging you. Begin again right now. Are you breathing? I mean, can you still fog a mirror? Great. Then yes, YOU can begin again.

Push away the **Regrets**

Push away the **Anger**

Push away the **Fear**

Push away the **Blame**

Push away the **Lies of the enemy**

Push away the **Habit of Procrastination**

Push away the **Guilt**

Push away the **Un-forgiveness**

Push away the **Excuses**

It is NOT too late!

GREEN FLAG TIME – *ReStart – Begin Again*

"I can do ALL things through Christ

who gives me strength"

Philippians 4:13

YELLOW FLAG: **HAZARDOUS** *situation, slow down*

Men, you have experienced many times of danger and hazardous situations. Those periods of pain, uncertainty and grief have provided you with a knowledge that you can overcome such deep, dark valleys. You have also witnessed friends and family members sailing through their own turbulent waters. This should hearten you and give you the courage to keep moving ahead in the face of these inevitable hardships.

The real threat of "Yellow Flag" periods is not slowing down and being cautious when the hazards or hardships appear. The biggest threat is not getting back up to your "Racing Speed" when danger has passed on. You have to get on with your life at the high performance speed you were meant to live. Staying in the yellow flag, slow and cautious mode, is damaging painful and unhealthy. Airplanes are said to wear out faster while sitting on the ground versus flying the friendly skies. Airplanes were specifically engineered to fly.

Horses are at their best when running with their cowboy companion. It's time to get back on that horse and ride, Cowboy! Giddy-Up my friend.

RED FLAG: **DANGER**, *the race stops immediately*

The RED Flag of Danger is much more serious than the Yellow Flag of caution. The RED Flag is a signal of a clear and present danger that stops all racers in their tracks. Something big and bad has occurred and everything grinds to a screeching halt until the situation is rectified.

You have experienced these life events from time to time. However, they never seem to come at an expected or opportune time. These are quick jolts of lightning that we know are inevitable. It seems we are never quite prepared for their intrusion into our comfortable lives. These are painful but not uncommon to all men.

Perhaps an elderly parent has taken ill and requires immediate medical care. Maybe it's a brother or sister that just tested positive for cancer or another very serious illness. Perhaps a very close friend or relative is suddenly cast into the middle of a very bitter and painful divorce.

These are real and present RED Flags of serious Danger and Heartache hitting us in the face. Relentless pain and unavoidable direct action has to be taken on our part. We can't just slow down and go about our daily business as if nothing ever happened. This is serious and it must be dealt with head on.

Danger and Fear must be met head on and dealt with firmly. Your response should be as swift as possible to minimize the pain and suffering.

The Buffalo and Cattle Approach

I recently read the account of how Buffalo and Cattle living on the Plains of western America approach Danger and Fear in totally opposite ways. This is a very interesting case we should consider in our lives. How do you approach serious issues?

It is said that when a huge thunderstorm builds, in the sky, and begins to release its' fury on the Plains, a very unique reaction and scenario is played out. It starts with fierce lightning flashes, the heavy thunder rolling, and the strong winds howling. It's at this point the herds of animals start moving. Immediately the storms' massive rains beat down on the plains and its' inhabitants.

What do the Cattle do? *Cattle quickly begin running away from the impending storm and all its' fury. The moving storm then catches up to the cattle and overtakes them.*

As the cattle continue to try running away from the storm it engulfs them and beats upon them with a relentless barrage. The storms punishment lasts much longer than the cattle would like and way longer than is necessary.

REALLY? *Hold that thought.*

What do the Buffalo do *in this same storm?*

Now, let's study those actions of the stately wild buffalo of the great plains. In the midst of this horrific and powerful great plains thunderstorm we can observe the attitude and the movement of the buffalo.

Unlike the cattle, the buffalo promptly turn and take the storm head on. That's right. The buffalo actually face the approaching storm. What they do next is quite amazing. The buffalo now facing the violent weather begin to charge into the brunt of it. What a courageous and unique approach to the Danger and Fear that is before them.

With this instinctive maneuver the buffalo are actually exposed to the storms' fury for a much shorter period of time.

Fascinating approach isn't it? AND *Those actions, by the buffalo, are also credited with taking them through and safely to the backside of the storm well before the cattle. Running with the storm the cattle extend their suffering and abuse from the weather.*

MEN, *when the* RED *Flag of* Danger *and* Fear *waves; are you running away with the* Cattle *or are your* Charging Head On *with the* Buffalo.

My money says we need to start enjoying the advantages of the Buffalo mindset.

BLACK FLAG: **STOP NOW** *and return to Pit area*

The BLACK FLAG *is truly the most serious signal of the whole series. Yes, Black is the traditional color of death and ultimate sorrow. When the Black Flag rears its' ugly head in our life we are shocked.* EVERYTHING *instantly stops. Life as we know it is altered or changed forever. The life that we enjoyed or experienced, only moments before, is swept away at the blink of an eye. Shock and instant sorrow often accompany these dreaded revelations of death and loss. It happens when we least expect it. It comes like a thief in the night.*

For you know very well that the Lord will come like a thief in the night.

1 Thess. 2

We can't truly prepare or rehearse for these black scenes of life. Tragedy of this magnitude is never gentle or kind. It is blunt, cold and unfeeling.

It just...........is.

BLACK FLAG *Pain can be excessive and certainly overwhelming. This pain is magnified for a man in my position. The life I live lends itself to an overabundance of quality relationships. This becomes a double edged sword and in turn I am exposed to an overabundance of heartache.*

I'm a man of nearly endless friendships. Like my father, I have never met a stranger. The only friends I don't have today are the people around the globe I have yet to meet. Blessed with many years of life I have also been gifted with core strengths of Positivity, Connection, Empathy, WOO (winning others over) and Communication. These first 5 core strengths are confirmed according to scientific testing by the World renown Gallup Organization.

This base of skills has served me quite well and allowed a richness in me that money can't buy. Over decades, I have shared special moments and bonded quite easily with thousands of wonderful people. I count each of these as my friends.

I have always been the glue-man of any group. I have the uncanny knack to bond quickly with quality people of nearly any extreme. In any social setting I seem to quickly become "everybody's" friend. I'm not saying I agree with everything they stand for. I tell people, "Heck, I don't even agree with myself on everything". It's not about equally shared values. It is about equally shared respect, kindness and civility.

I've been married going on 4 decades and I have repeatedly told my wife I would gladly do it all over again. We have had an exceptional marriage and life together. No doubt we are envied by many. However, my wife and I have countless differences of opinion.

Our likes and dislikes vary wildly at times. We just blend it all together and prove that variety is certainly a spice in our life.

I have always worked to truly make honest connections. If you are a good person I like meeting and mingling with you in a non-superficial way. I have always excelled at a position of kindness, respect and genuine interest. (We are not talking about socializing with evil and nasty wretches of human beings here.)

People that spend only a few minutes with me realize that I am certainly not a jellyfish of a man. I am not one with squishy, slimy and ever-changing values and convictions. That is certainly not who I am. That is the position displayed by countless politicians of our day. I am a solid man of very deeply held convictions. I have always burned strong with a firm sense of justice for right and wrong in people and their actions.

PLEASE, *My above personal descriptive notations are not to be seen as prideful statements but facts as I've experienced them.* Actually, *I wish to express these statements as points of true gratitude and with an extremely full and thankful heart.*

Your BLACK Flag *can come in the form of death to a life partner. Often this* Black Flag *event cuts a wound so deep and wide that it takes years to get back on track. Maybe years to reach even a fraction of past peak performance speed. Timing for this specific recovery is certainly beyond my level of competence. It is truly unique to every persons' circumstances. I know from many dear friends that it is all a matter of time and processing. Grieving of such magnitude is neither quick or easy. It is also not to be avoided, denied or suppressed. It must be felt, fought through and endured.*

I have, from time to time, contemplated my response and life-after scenario at the untimely passing of my wonderful wife. These visions of my "after- Glenda-Life" are a combination of frightening, painful, unfocused and unnerving. I have tried to discuss our funeral and passing arrangements, with her, dozens of times, and I can't get her to engage for more than a glancing minute. This is a painful issue for her and a lot of people. Just yesterday I tried to explain that a family gripped by the grief, of her passing, should not be placed in a situation of making a series of emotional and important decisions.

MEN,

Please, be a man, and take care of business in this area of your life. Don't make a bad situation worse.

You owe it to your family to have these arrangements planned out and settled well before this unavoidable event occurs.

My friend Jeff Goldberg, is hilarious and very direct. He says it is a known fact that 100% of the people born before 1899, have died. Thanks Jeff. You see. No one gets out of this place alive.

MEN, it is When – Not IF. Do It Now!

You may also experience a Black Flag through the passing of a sibling or elderly parent. As of this writing my dad has passed. Both of Glenda's parents have also passed on. Thankfully her brother and my siblings are still with us.

My sister Myra was a whisper away from death just a few years back. A drunk driver ran a red light in southern California and nearly took her away from us. The Doctor called her his "Miracle" girl. Myra always was stubborn and you couldn't make her do anything she didn't want to do. I guess she didn't want to leave us right then.

She is an amazing person and purely a shining example of God's Faith, Hope and Love. Oh, if we could all strive to be more like Myra. Not the stubborn part, but the Faith, Hope and Love side.

One form of life's BLACK Flag, that I can't even fathom, is the crushing blow of losing a child well before they have truly lived. I absolutely don't understand the magnitude of pain and sorrow associated with this kind of loss. As a parent I would instantly, and without any hesitation, give my life to save my children, Adam or Sarah.

I recall a few years back my son Adam and his lovely wife Brooke were living in their first home. About 6 months after they moved in, they experienced a major plumbing failure that required a lot of money for repairs. Being his loving dad, I was the first emergency rescue call he made. He quickly laid out the problem at hand. He also explained how expensive the required repairs would be.

You could tell in his voice that he was quite shaken. I knew right away that the amount of repair money required was not within their grasp. I quickly assured him that his mother and I would handle the cost of repairs. I let him know that he should not let this problem create an excessive burden or worry him.

Instantly, like the pin prick to a full party balloon, I could audibly hear, and physically feel, the tension and anxiety release from his body. It was quite an amazing exchange from a son to his father.

A *few days later* Adam *revealed to me how amazed he was at the non-hesitant response* I *made to his serious financial hurdle.* He *knew we were still passing through some turbulent financial waters ourselves. That fact, of course, made my response more powerful.* I *simply looked at* Adam *and said;*

"Son, I will always help you. To my Last Penny, To my Last Breath. I will help you"

I told Adam during our continuing discussion that when he had children, of his own, then he too would fully understand the depth of a parent's love and devotion to their child. If you remember chapter 1 about "Harper Lee at 3" then you already know that Adam and Brooke have joined the love filled world of parenting. Praise God for Grandchildren. They are fabulous ☺.

One final point in our Black Flag session is something I can discuss first hand. I personally have experienced the agonizing death in the form of a total financial collapse. This was the result of a perfect storm. Ingredients of that perfect storm were numerous and now quite obvious. They included, but were not limited to, impeccable credit, overwhelming positivity, unbridled pride and the biggest financial meltdown of the century.

I joke that I only came out the other end with the clothes on my back and my brains. However, my brains were totally scrambled like a batch of breakfast eggs. Talk about putting your Pride in a vice and squeezing out the very last drop. Ugh, Double Ugh!

What doesn't kill you.......will make your stronger. But often in the middle of it......you will wish for death.
Dave Wadsworth

I don't see myself as arrogant, by nature, but I have an abundance of the sin called PRIDE that often plagues me. I have always been a proud person and I know we should all possess a healthy "seasoned" amount, of pride, to function normally as human beings.

A person totally devoid of pride is unequipped and functioning in a harmful emotional position. A person with excessive amounts, of Pride, are repulsive at best.

These Pride-bloated individuals are for sure dangerous to themselves and others. Pride, like most ingredients in life, should be utilized more as a seasoning than the staple. Too much salt will make you immediately gag and vomit. Too little, or no salt, will leave life bland and unnecessarily weak.

"Too much of a GOOD thing.........is a BAD thing"
"Too little of a GOOD thing...........is a Bad thing"
Dave Wadsworth

I'm thrilled to report that my business and family survived this financial "valley-of-death". We are now back on track and thriving. When in the depths of darkness and despair you have to keep telling yourself that **"THIS TOO...... SHALL PASS"** *and it will.*

I do have to give a big shout out to 4 men in particular that were extremely vital in my safe passage through this very rough patch.

Mr. Dan Miller my dear friend and mentor. His words and encouraging podcasts were amazing. What a true gift and treasure for humanity he is. I do have to credit a lot of Dan's success to his beautiful, graceful and sweet spirited wife ***Joanne.*** **"PURE CLASS"**

Ken Idleman *our preacher at Crossroads Christian Church. One of the finest gentlemen I have ever met in my life. Ken, how did you know to preach all those sermons directly to me? It was as if I was the only one, in the auditorium, and you were speaking directly into my heart. That was* **MIRACULOUS.**

Doug Wadsworth, the 3rd most wonderful man I've ever known. A friend and brother like no other. God made you special and my life has literally been in your hands many times. I LOVE YOU.

I can't leave out my best friend Carl Westfall. The king of crazy, sarcasm and the occasional backhanded compliment. Every Saturday morning, we would meet in Newburgh for prayer and breakfast. Setting across the table the following image was permanently etched into my mind. Carl would passionately and emotionally get in my face. With his, quite animated, hand, body and facial gestures he would say the same thing over and over and over again.

"I promise you....I promise you....I promise you ....this will get better. You-will-be-ok.

Although Carl never gave or loaned me any money (tight-wad) through all of this; what he did give me was much more valuable. Thanks Brother, I love you. (and not in a creepy way)

Dawn, since Carl probably won't read this book please don't tell him this stuff and swell his head. 😊

BLACK & WHITE CHECKERED FLAG

Hey Dave. You forgot the White Flag. Just simmer down and keep your shirt on. I'll get there very soon.

Again, since you are reading this book it is plain that you are not finished with your race yet. Hey, what an astute observation on my part. My book title is "Finishing" on Fire and that obviously indicates Action and a degree of Incompleteness.

MEN, *whatever your age. Where ever you are in your particular race of life. This book is providing you with inspiration, ideas and tools to implement here and now. Without delay your whole life and outlook should and could change. Start making those choices* HERE *and* NOW.

WHITE FLAG: FINAL LAP MEN

Gentlemen.....

START...........YOUR........ENGINES!!!

Men often die as early as their 40's......... and their body just keeps on functioning until many decades later when it physically gives out. -Unknown

ANSWER THESE QUESTIONS, MEN,

Are you just going through the motions?
Have you already died but your body hasn't been told yet?
Are you living in a rut?
(RUT – *defined as a grave with both ends knocked out*)
Are you wandering without Purpose?
Are you "living" without Passion?
Is True Prosperity absent in your life?
Is your living truly......."lifeless"?

In one of his books I heard Bob Proctor discussing men and their thinking habits. Bob tells about how men go through the motions like zombies and don't even engage in any serious thinking. He said:

"2% of all men think"
"3% of all men think they think" and
"95% would rather die than think"
-Bob Proctor

Bob, continues with a quote from the legendary Earl Nightingale "if most men said what they were thinking.......They would be speechless"

How sad is that commentary on man? Living a life as a wandering and directionless sheep-of-a-man is not true living.

Auto pilot for our cars, planes and trains is certainly acceptable. It is probably even a wise feature for safety sake. Auto pilot for your life is a pathetic disaster of a life. That is not life. That is not living. That is mere existence.

I really love the movie **"Second Hand Lions"** *starring Robert Duvall and Michael Caine. It is flat-out hilarious at times. Although it is truly funny, it is laced with some very sound points of living life on fire. This movie is required viewing for participants of our two- day 12-man workshop called Finishing on Fire.*

At the end of the movie, the great nephew Walter, played by Josh Lucas has the line that sums it all up. He is standing with the local sheriff looking at the end of a barn. The barn has an old WW I airplane smashed into the end of it. The old double-winged plane is upside down with the tail sticking out the end of the barn. It was the final resting place of his 2 wild hearted 90-year old uncles.

As the nephew (Walter) and sheriff are contemplating the wild and crazy accident; a very sleek and huge helicopter hovers in for a landing. A wealthy Arabic oil man and his young son step out and look around with amazement. The Oil man explains brieifly about his family and the wild stories involving the 2 uncles and their middle-eastern adventures. This ties up some loose ends but here is the real punch line.

The little boy looks at the plane and asked his father with amazement "So, you mean that the 2 men from great grandfather's stories really lived?"

At that question Josh Lucas' demeanor turned contemplative and he looked at the boy with a sincere gaze and with the expression of his whole body he says

"Yes............THEY. REALLY. LIVED. "

Gentlemen, that's what I'm talking about 😊

8. HAVE VISION OR PERISH

Where there is no VISION…the people Perish.

Proverbs 29:18

Jack Nicholson and Morgan Freeman star in the blockbuster movie "THE BUCKET LIST". This is one of my all-time favorite movies and I highly recommend that you watch it. This also is required viewing for all participants in our 2-Day Workshop entitled "Finishing on Fire". Having a "Bucket List", of your own, is an important part of you living a Healthy, Wealthy and Wise life.

Action Item - Bucket List

It is time for you to do something you have always believed to be naughty, disrespectful and wrong. I want you to write in this book. Oh, yes. Write in this book. It's yours and to get the most out of it you have to write out your thoughts and plans.

MY BUCKET LIST --- RULES OR GUIDELINES

Write out your Top 10 "Bucket List" Items.
List 10 items that are life experiences you have never had but would really, really like to partake in.
They can be solo or as a couple or group.

Money is NO Object.

Time is NO Object.

Health is NO Object.

1. ____________________

2. ____________________

3. ____________________

4. ____________________

5. ____________________

6. ____________________

7. ____________________

8. ____________________

9. ____________________

10. ____________________

BUCKET LIST TOP 5

Now pare down the list to your top 5.

1. ____________________
2. ____________________
3. ____________________
4. ____________________
5. ____________________

BUCKET LIST TOP 3

Now cut list to your top 3

1. ____________________
2. ____________________
3. ____________________

BUCKET LIST TOP 3 --- DETAILS

GUIDELINES

Write the Bucket List Item

Write Date at which you plan to complete it

Write names of Who will be with you

Write location and how you will get there

Write details about the activities

Write details about the food there

Write weather details

BUCKET LIST # 1

List item ______________________________

Item Date ______________________________

Who? Write Names of People Involved

____

____

Write Location and How You will get There

Write Details about Activities

Write Details about the Food There

Write Details about the Weather

BUCKET LIST # 2

List item ______________________________

Item Date ______________________________

Who? Write Names of People Involved

____

____

Write Location and How You will get There

____

____

____

Write Details about Activities

____

____

____

Write Details about the Food There

Write Details about the Weather

BUCKET LIST # 3

List item ____________________

Item Date ____________________

Who? Write Names of People Involved

____

____

Write Location and How You will get There

____

____

____

Write Details about Activities

____

____

____

Write Details about the Food There

Write Details about the Weather

By writing in as many Bucket List item details as possible you are actually solidifying the reality of that item coming to life.

9. PURGE THE POISON

Key to Finishing ON Fire:

Dumping The BAGGAGE

Your Mind is a Garden

Your Thoughts are the Seeds

You can Grow Flowers

Or

You can Grow Weeds

If you are going to continue your journey in life, you must lighten the load. I have a tendency to collect and carry excessive baggage. My wife calls me a "Hoarder". What? That's so hurtful. I promise I am not a "Hoarder". I do admit that I can be classified as a Pack Rat!! Huge difference.

I have been in the homes of hoarders and it is "unbelievable". When I was an industrious young boy I was employed to carry 3 separate paper routes in our small town. One was our daily local paper that I carried 6 days per week. Another was the huge (5 lbs. each) Sunday morning paper. The Sunday morning, massive advertising paper required pedaling my bike for miles in the cold, dark, and deserted streets of predawn Plainville. The other route was a monthly called "The Grit".

An elderly gentlemen, we'll just call Mr. Z, lived near the tail end of my daily paper route. Mr. Z lived alone at the end of the street. His house was located near the elementary school by our little league baseball fields. He was a friendly and peculiar fellow who mostly kept to himself. His yard and home were surrounded with endless piles of junk and debris.

Lawn mowers of every make, model and size. A rainbow of colors from the various brands. Each mower appeared to have something not quite right with it. A wheel that was flat or missing. An engine torn apart. The seat or handle bars broken. Every mower or item thrown about the yard looked like it should have been on Rudolph's island of misfit toys.

Basically there was just a path to walk through Mr. Z's yard and around the outside of his house. I'm not sure why he even had all those mowers. Nearly every square inch of his lot was covered with junk. Where could the grass have room to grow anyway?

Of course his front porch was swamped with piles and piles of.........stuff. I did remember seeing a number of cats that he kept around. I'm pretty sure the mice population would have kept them all fed without Mr. Z even spending a dime on cat food.

On a rare occasion I was invited to step into this man's home. I never felt uneasy or endangered at any time. Running my paper business required me to collect the payment for past paper deliveries. My parents raised me to be kind and respectful of everyone. I believe I did a pretty good job of keeping to that high standard. Even shocked by the abundant nasty mess I hope I never disrespected Mr. Z during our encounters.

Thinking back, I must have been a boy about the age of 12 when I first met this gentleman and his "jungle of junk". The outside was so full of junk he could barely pull his car onto his property.

Just like it was yesterday I can remember my heart skipped a beat and my eyes must have been the size of saucers as I first stepped foot in his home. I thought the outside was nothing but a mice infested ridiculous junkyard.

Well, the inside was 10 times worse and smelled like musty paper and rotten garbage. Piles and piles of newspapers and magazines were everywhere. I hadn't seen that much printed material at our local library. The piles inside his home seemed to stretch from floor to ceiling. They were packed together to fill the room in a very haphazard way. I do remember a kitchen chair and the corner of a table exposed just enough to allow Mr. Z to sit down and read his paper.

I remember I really only had room to stand in the entryway to Mr. Z's house. From what I could tell, Mr. Z had a good sized home. Once inside it was just piles and piles of stuff. There was only a series of trails or narrow paths to walk about from room to room. Although I liked Mr. Z, he was clearly a "HOARDER" of the first order.

One last point on Mr. Z was his car. Or should I say cars. I forgot to mention that he probably had 2 or 3 junk cars strewn among the junk and weeds. These were in various positions of disrepair just like the lawnmowers. The one working vehicle Mr. Z would drive about town suffered the same fate as his home and "yard". That car was stuffed with........stuff. I don't know how he had room to get groceries and find a place to pack them home in that car. Excessive Baggage for sure.

I know, I know. You are thinking that Mr. Z is a fool. No "normal" person would be hanging on to that burdensome and useless baggage. You just read about all the excessive baggage that Mr. Z has accumulated. You also rightly agreed at how ridiculous this is. He should start discarding all that broken and useless junk. It is just a needless anchor around his neck. It is something that he could throw away with a little extra effort. I can't really disagree with you on those points.

Here is the truth about your common bond with Mr. Z.

In many ways you are a mirrored image of Mr. Z.

Yes, you are. I know that sounds blasphemous and ludicrous to you but hear me out.

YOUR INVISIBLE BAGGAGE

Since you were a young child you have been accumulating excessive baggage. That baggage is dirty, smelly, unsightly and heavy. It is new, old and all broken and useless. Most of it is hidden from the view or knowledge of others. Sometimes you even lose sight or memory of it yourself. However, you still keep it, and even collect more each day. You are letting it hold you back from reaching your peak performance speed in life. Consider the following list of garbage and nasty baggage you have accumulated and refuse to properly dispose of:

PURGE *the* POISON

REGRETS

FEAR

ANGER

HATRED

JEALOUSY

REVENGE

BITTERNESS

UNFORGIVENESS

BAD HABITS

BAD THOUGHTS

NEGATIVE THOUGHTS

and

LIST OTHERS YOU HAVE BELOW

I'm telling you that your heavy, smelly useless baggage and garbage is many times worse than Mr. Z.

Your mess is all crammed into your mind, heart and soul.
Dave Wadsworth

KeyQuote: MEN, PLEASE HEAR ME ON THIS
Anger, Regrets, Bitterness, Hatred, Unforgiveness, Jealousy & Revenge only damage and destroy the container that carries them>>> YOU
Dave Wadsworth

You have to dump the baggage and garbage to truly begin living life. Choose to live Garbage free and Finish on Fire.

Men, *Please* PURGE *your* POISON – NOW

ACTION ITEM: *Above, Write out the negative people you struggle with. Write out the negative issues you struggle with. Focus on forgiveness with each of these people. Focus on dumping each of the negative issues.*

Hanging on to baggage and garbage only hurts you. Start dumping the garbage to make room for all the good stuff coming your way. I promise you that just filling in the blanks is a huge jumpstart to lightening your load.

DUMP IT NOW!!!

10. DEAD BY MIDNIGHT

ACTION ITEM: *This will change your life.*

This scenario is from a book I read and I'm pretty sure the credit goes to the fabulous Og Mandino.

So many times we judge, criticize and condemn people flippantly. We have little or no regard for their lives or magnitude of things they are dealing with. I've heard it said that based on full knowledge we would make similar decisions as the people we are criticizing. If we were totally immersed in their footsteps we would likely fall prey to making those same poor choices. We need to remember that our entire lives are built upon a series of endless choices. Most are small and cause very minor incremental changes. I'd also like to point out that people decide most everything in regard to their best interest. This best interest is many times taking the lesser of two evils.

"FORREST GUMP" – *Starring Tom Hanks is a true favorite of mine. The mentally slow boy grows to manhood and teaches everyone solid lessons in common decency and human respect. How he views and thus treats everyone he engages is truly remarkable. Forrest views people with innocent eyes, a kind heart and childlike love. With a very simple mind, Forrest teaches fundamentally premium communication.*

Men, we can all take valuable lessons from an "idiot" like Forrest Gump.

INSTRUCTIONS: *"Dead By Midnight"* Action Item

You can make a game of this or approach it in any way you like. Starting immediately, you need to pretend that you have a deep dark secret. This secret is not to be revealed but you must act as if it is the solid truth.

The secret is that everyone you meet and engage is going to be dead by midnight tonight. No exceptions. Think about that for a minute and let the idea soak into your mind and heart.

Now, as you meet the first person of the day take your mind back to that secret about that person. They are totally unaware of their own impending death. You however know the secret of their serious position. You can view them in this light and treat them with genuine acknowledgement, respect and kindness. Tomorrow they will be dead and their family grieving the loss. How many times do we go through the day and ignore or insult dozens of people because of our own arrogance and self-righteousness. When you first start "seeing" these people it will seem weird but kind of mystical.

I promise that this one simple communications technique will change your life.

You will be amazed at how enlightening this will be for other people. Everyone wants to be noticed, respected and treated with kindness. You do. This simple action will absolutely light people up. It will turn them on to you in a powerful way. I can guarantee a generous response will nearly always come back your way.

I challenge you to try this for 1 week. Your life will be enhanced exponentially. It doesn't cost you 1 red cent. But, it can be worth a fortune to you. I guarantee your spirit will be buoyed to a level you haven't felt in years, or maybe ever.

***I promise you**. If you do nothing else but implement this one technique:*

YOUR LIFE WILL EXPLODE *in*

Purpose Passion & Prosperity!

11. POWER IN BEING THERE

Reading (& listening to) some 2,000 books the past 4 years has been inspiring, enjoyable and enlightening. However, the numerous "Live Events" I have also attended, during this period, have been irreplaceable in my quest for knowledge, wisdom and high-value relationships.

Jim Rohn often quoted Charlie "Tremendous" Jones who said "In 5 years you will be the same person you are today, except for:

1. The people you meet
2. The books you read"

These live events have afforded me the opportunity to have lunch with and converse with numerous high quality people including a number of billionaires.

Engaging in multiple masterminds has also allowed me the pleasure of weekly learning and discussion opportunities with dozens of millionaires. I have purposely sought out these live personal interactions. I intentionally target people of the highest moral character and generous value systems that I also hold dear.

"It is always hard to Soar like an Eagle, when You are surrounded by Turkeys!!"

That is one of my basic and all-time favorite quotes. Look for the "abundance" mentality people who soar as eagles and are thrilled to be a part of teaching you how to do the same.

Pursue Eagles that will teach you to soar. My dear friend Dan Miller is just such an Eagle of the highest character. Check out his many books, especially his New York Times Best Selling Book "48 Days to the Work You Love".

Dan and his lovely wife Joanne are my mentors and encouragers of the highest degree. They display an unmatched spirit of love, generosity and moral character.

Masterminds are also a huge part of my personal growth. If you want more details about masterminds, please read a classic called "Think and Grow Rich" by Napoleon Hill. You can also follow another friend of mine from Nashville, TN, Aaron Walker. He has phenomenal information on masterminds and leadership materials on his website entitled "View from the Top". Aaron also has built an incredible base of men's masterminds under the title of "Iron Sharpens Iron". Certainly a man of quality I wholeheartedly recommend.

When it comes to self-improvement, I can honestly say that I have not met anyone who has invested more in both time and dollars than myself. I have been relentless in my pursuit of knowledge, wisdom and high-value relationships.

Thus, I can unreservedly say if you truly want to Finish your life on Fire you should attend one of our 2 day in-person workshops. Your investment of time and money, in yourself, will easily bring you a multiple return in value.

Finishing on Fire 2-day workshops are held all over the world and hosted by myself and our professional team. We welcome only MEN of the highest character, or MEN who aspire to be, MEN of the highest character. These workshops are hard-hitting, no holds barred and truly life changing action packed events. Finishing on Fire workshops take men through a transformational process unlike any other they have experienced.

This book takes you through some of that "workshop journey". **WARNING:** *Reading a book is no substitute for the life changing experience of a live event. I personally can't put a price on the high-value relationships I have forged through live events and their related activities.*

Finishing on Fire 2-day Workshops are purposely held to a maximum of 12 men participants. This allows extreme positive transformations to occur. A bonus of the 12-man cap is greater relationship forging with fellow high-value participants and the Finishing on Fire Leadership Team. Guaranteed personal growth and bonding opportunities are yours for the taking. Purpose, Passion and Prosperity values in these new relationships alone will significantly multiply your initial investment.

Finishing on Fire workshops are not just Flowers and Sunshine Rah, Rah sessions. Our workshops take you on a transformational journey of Action, Facts, Feelings, Foundations, Friendships and Concrete Formulas of Success. You will leave with a solid game plan for daily living the life you have always desired. Your new life filled with Purpose, Passion and Prosperity. Your new Legacy Life of Faith, Family and Freedom.

Continuing Finishing on Fire "participant only" masterminds are available if so desired. These masterminds provide focus, friendships and sustained accountability to the Purpose, Passion & Prosperity level you desire.

Life is not a solo journey. Life is only lived fully alive by teaming with individuals and groups focused on building a better life, a better family, a better community and a better world for all.

We, are about the "abundance" mentality of each man made better, equals all men made better.

Dave Wadsworth

Again, we all decide how we live our lives. We can live in FEAR or in FAITH. An optimistic or hopeful person lives in faith every day. They look for the good in people. They look for the good in situations. They look for the good in themselves. They are glass half full people.

"There is always something positive you can find in any situation life brings your way."

Dave Wadsworth

"Whatever the situation, however dire it seems at first glance, there's always a bright side. And looking at the funny side releases tensions. It puts things into perspective, and opens the mind to possible solutions."

P. Lindsay

12. TARGET PEOPLE

ACTION ITEM: *Target People*

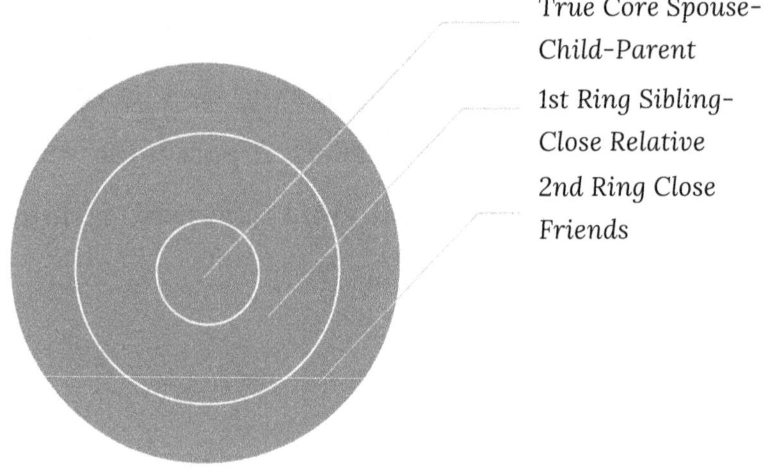

I have a fantastic wife, mother, adult son and adult daughter. My daughter-in-law and son-in-law are first rate human beings. My siblings and extended family are all very high quality people.

"There are people in this world who would pay millions of dollars to enjoy the fabulous family relationships that I have."

Dave Wadsworth

That is just the riches I have in my family. My friendships are monumental in value above and beyond my family.

If you want a piece of my relationship riches I will gladly help you get there.

Call Me @ 812-499-5090 .

Seriously, pick up the phone and call me.

Or you can just Read on and Engage.

This chapter will challenge you to focus on and evaluate your critical relationships. We often take for granted the people who we truly love the most. These are the CORE people in our lives. They have been with us the longest in most cases. They will also stay with us the longest. They will be there when everyone else has fallen away and moved on with their lives.

Finishing on Fire requires healthy relationships!!

By now, you have cleaned out all your garbage. Or, at least you are moving strongly to do so. I'm hoping you also released your own personal baggage. **Remember?** *Regrets, Anger, Un-forgiveness, Bitterness, Hatred etc.*

If you have not cleaned your own house, you can't start into the next phase. Focus on **you** *until the poison has been purged from your heart and mind. You can't keep your poisonous past around like it is no big deal. IT IS A BIG DEAL. Vomit that disgusting past out of you.*

Once you have cleaned your house it's time to move ahead into developing or rebuilding your core relationships.

You always start with your spouse since she is # 1. If she is not number one, then you have to develop a game plan to get that changed. This is the person you pledged your life to. At one time you were over the moon in love with them. They also felt the same about you. Take your mind back to those "glory" days. Remind yourself of who you are and who they are. Successfully Finishing on Fire requires a strong and happy marriage. After 35 years of marriage I can promise you one thing:

If you treat your wife like a "thoroughbred" she won't turn into an "old Nag"

If that one, went over your head just contact a horse person and they will explain it to you.

"If you treat your wife". This is all on you. It is something you have 100% control of. Her response is not in your control. How you treat her IS within your control.

Many times we use our wife as a verbal punching bag or dumping ground. We justify it by saying "I have to talk to someone". I SAY BULL!! *We all have to unload our tension and frustrations in a reasonable and civil manner. Our spouse doesn't deserve a daily barrage of our letting off steam. She wasn't the cause and yet she gets the verbal smack-down.* STOP IT!!

There are lots of ways to deal with life's frustrations rather than mentally bashing your wife with them. Get the help you need personally. Then get the proper help you both need as a couple.

Hey Dude, you are in the 4th quarter of your life. Time to *fix this thing and* DO LIFE RIGHT.

If you have a living parent, today is the time to also clean up that mess. Stop waiting on them to apologize or come to their senses of a past wrong or offense. Man up and mend any fences that are weak or broken down completely. They will soon be gone and you will have chocked up another huge regret. A very unnecessary regret.

I never ask or expect anyone to stay in an abusive, hostile or dangerous relationship. If you are being abused, threatened or feel you are in eminent danger – PLEASE -- Get Out *as soon as possible.*

ACTION ITEM: PEOPLE TARGET TIME

BULLSEYE – CORE PEOPLE

List the name of your Spouse first. Then list all your children. Finally list any living parent.

1st Ring – Siblings & Close Relatives

List the names of your Siblings first.
Now list all your close relatives Nephews
Nieces Aunts Uncles Cousins.

1st Ring – Siblings & Close Relatives Cont.

2nd Ring – Close Friends

List the names of your Close Friends

ACTION ITEM

BULLSEYE – CORE PEOPLE

TARGET LETTERS *of* NEW LIFE

Do this one action item and your life will never be the same. If your marriage is good, it will get better. If a child or parent is estranged, the ICE might begin to crack. Good stuff will come from this.

NO FEAR – NO EXCUSES = NO REGRETS

THIS IS A BIGGIE 😊

Ok, here is the assignment. Write a letter to each of the Bullseye, Core people on your list. Spouse first, Children Second (all children) then living parents.

SCENARIO: *You have 24 hours to live.*

Guaranteed you will be dead. No second chances here. Now, write the letter and say what you need to say.

Seriously. Write as if these are your very last words to this person. I mean you lay it all out there. Speak as if there is NO tomorrow. Guess what? There is NO tomorrow. Specifically Apologize for the things that made her cry (if you can remember them all). I promise it will make her cry again. For good this time. Tell her truly what she has meant to you over these years. Cite specific examples of things she did or said that really made you feel like a man.

You can tell her in the letter what this assignment is so she won't totally freak out. **RULES** *– Only the good stuff. No negative jabs or slaps. You have already tried the ugly stuff. It didn't do you any good the first time. This could be the most important and relationship changing communication in your marriage. Write this letter in your own handwriting. Sign this letter. Date this letter.*

MAIL THIS LETTER TO HER.

This Will Rock Her World........And Yours.

Next week write the same scenario letter to your children. The second week write the letter to your parents.

Hang on Brother, you are on your way to some surprising and amazing relationship changes.

13. 4TH QUARTER...GET IN THE GAME

Running back on offense, cornerback on defense, punt returner and kickoff receiver. Wow, I was a busy boy. I love, love, love football. Broken thumb, broken finger, broken collarbone, bruised kidney, strained Achilles tendon etc. I absolutely loved playing the game. Sunshine, rain, sleet and ice. I loved the teamwork and comradery. The struggle through pain and on to victory. Not always a victor, on the scoreboard, but when we pulled together as one true unit, I always felt we were winners. We gave it our best shot and each battle further cemented that bond of true brothers.

The North Daviess High School Cougars were building a respectable program through my playing days. Our senior class set the school win record. Next year my brother Doug's class bested that mark.

A few years later they were a few ticks away from playing for a state championship. Oh, those glory days. It's hard to beat those hard fought battles with your band of buddies.

The fans, the band, and the gridiron battle made for fantastic memories. I loved running the football and scoring touchdowns. Most of the games were hard fought and fairly close encounters. One thing I always remember was our endless running in practice. I remember always holding something back to make it through those final practice sprinting sessions.

The coaches wanted us to have plenty of fuel, in the tank, when the 4th quarter rolled around. Wow, the 4th quarter of football on Friday night. It all came down to this. The first 3 quarters were like body blows and dancing around for position. The 4th quarter is where it became do or die time. Put up or shut up.

I love watching college football on TV. The spirit and enthusiasm is incredible. All the excitement and suspense continually builds until the 4th quarter whistle blows. That's when the players all hold up 4 fingers to indicate it's GO TIME!!! *Now or never time for you to take care of business. Men, we have no 5th quarter.*

Men, It's your 4th Quarter.

It's NOW *or* NEVER.

It's GO *time* Gentlemen.

Get *in the* Game!!

It's *Time to Play*!

No REGRETS - No EXCUSES - No FEAR

No *Reservations* – No *Retreat* – No *Do-overs*

14. TELL PEOPLE......ON?

To Finish on Fire you are going to have to make significant changes to your thinking, speaking and actions. Break with your old paradigms that are no longer true, necessary or nice.

I used to tell my students to always ask themselves 3 important questions before they speak. These questions could mean great value to them in their everyday existence.

Before opening your mouth, you should silently ask "is what I'm about to say ---

1. Is it True?

2. Is it Necessary?

3. Is it Nice?

If the answer to any of these three questions is NO; that is probably a good indication that you should keep your mouth shut.

Do you remember hearing people brag about how they just told somebody OFF? They really gave them a piece of their mind. Usually that person didn't have much of a mind to spare (hey, you were thinking it too 😊). Remember how important it seemed to make them feel. Remember how you thought, well that person certainly deserved a good tongue lashing.

But, you also were thinking.....Hmm.....I wonder if that is going to be worth it? I wonder how that is going to come back and bite them in the butt. I wonder if that wasn't just a stupid or immature knee-jerk reaction.

Nine times out of 10, the act of "chewing someone out" or "telling them OFF" turns into a regrettable mistake. A mistake that must be endured for a very long time. It becomes a hidden snake in the grass that often comes back to bite them in the end.

Men, here is an alternative lifestyle that will reap phenomenal results in a very short period of time. Don't tell people off! "TELL PEOPLE ON!!" What crazy idea is Telling People On about?

Success in life is about pushing people's buttons in a way that you can influence them for the good. Your genuine interactions can become a method of turning them ON (in a positive/non sexual way). Here is what I propose you start doing.

ACTION ITEM: TELL PEOPLE ON

When you meet someone, immediately look for an opportunity in the conversation to tell them what you think of them. Nice and genuine compliments are always welcome. People want to feel noticed. People want to feel important. People want to know that they are valued. Remember our "Dead by Midnight" technique. This runs in a similar vein. This could be that last time you see or speak to this person. Make a sincere effort to tell people exactly what you think of them. Connect, bond. Look them in the eye and say "do you remember when you did such n such for me?" That meant so very much. I really needed that. You can also give them a genuine compliment about how you always liked or admired "and name a quality they possess or an action that they did in the past". Always be positive and sincere. False flattery is Bull and Lying. False flattery and Lying is just drinking poison that you will just have to purge later. Don't do it and you won't have to vomit it back up later.

This "TELLING PEOPLE ON" technique will absolutely turn people and your relationships on!!

People won't always remember what you say.....But, they will always remember how you made them feel.
Maya Angelou

MEN, *tell people* ON.
It makes them feel good about themselves......and you.
BIG VALUE

BONUS: *Want a proven success technique in leadership and people management? Of course you do. Why else would you read this book.*

Correct people in private.
***Praise people in public.* ALWAYS!!!**

Always is strong wording but generally this is a very good practice.

15. MONEY MAGNIFIES

Millionaires and billionaires have generally worked hard and developed habits of doing the daily "little things" that others won't do. Small disciplines that seem insignificant will over time compound into massive success.

Through my focused 2,000 book reading (listening), this past 4 years, I have come to understand that it's not about the money.

"Money is just a Magnifier"

If you are a good person, money will enable you to do amazing positive things in a multiplied fashion. If you are a bad person, excessive money will reveal in you a dirty rotten bloated scoundrel.

Bob Proctor tells about a professional baseball player who confirmed this through his experiences. He told Bob that he knew many guys in the Minor Baseball Leagues who weren't nice guys. He went on to state that when these men got to the Major Leagues and signed those big multi-million dollar contracts, then these guys became almost unbearable. All the extra money just "highlighted" and "magnified" the true ugly nature of these people.

Money like a brick is amoral. It is neither good nor bad. Like a brick, money can be used for the cause of good or the cause of the wicked. Money can be used to build a church, a school, or a hospital for children. Money can also be used for reckless living and abusing people of lesser means. Money is simply a tool in the hand of a craftsman.

MEN, What positive work of art is your money creating?

16. FILLING YOUR JAR

CHOICES, CHOICES, CHOICES.

I read an interesting fact recently. It stated that our open eyes are constantly scanning the entire scene before us. With these scans our eyes and brain are jointly making over 11,000 choices per minute. As we enter a room we quickly scan for danger or pleasure. When we go into a theatre we don't count the chairs, no harm there. We do however notice the exits, how many and their locations. Driving our car, we consciously and subconsciously, scan and choose at the rate of hundreds of times per mile. We are keeping ourselves and others safe by choosing and driving through a series of constant and rapid adjustments. The brain is so very fascinating and we take it all for granted.

Andy Andrews talks about our life being built on an endless pile or collection of choices. He said we make choices and over time our choices make us. In his recent book "Bottom of The Pool" he goes a step deeper in his analysis. He said it is not our choices that determine who we are. He states that it is actually "Our Thinking" that determines who we are. He says it is our baseline thinking, that determines our choices, that determine our direction, that determines our actions, that ultimately determines "our life". I fully agree with Andy on this.

I however, want to take you to a point that I believe is a slight level deeper than our thinking. Viktor Frankl, who went through the vicious torture of the Auschwitz Nazi Death Camp, said that our last true freedom as a human being was "our Attitude". Our freedom to choose our own way in any situation. Our Attitude has the power of life or death. Attitude can make or break a family, a church, a community or a school.

It can make or break a team, a dream or a company.

It can make or break a city, a state or a nation.

Attitude is the Answer.

It all starts with **YOUR ATTITUDE**.

ATTITUDE *is the* ***key foundation stone*** *of your Life Success or failure.*

I firmly believe that it is your basic, positive or negative **"ATTITUDE"** *that determines your thinking.*

Your **ATTITUDE** *determines your thinking.*
Your **THINKING** *then determines your choices.*
Your **CHOICES** *then determine your direction.*
Your **DIRECTION** *then determines your actions.*
Your **ACTIONS** *ultimately determine..."Your Life".*

Action by Action our lives become this grand composite of OUR making. So, with a positive attitude I want you to come observe an interesting demonstration of philosophy.

JAR of BIG ROCKS

One day a teacher stood before his class with only a large glass jar sitting before him on the display table. The teacher said he wanted his students to participate in counting as he was filling this jar with large rocks.

The teacher pulled out a bag of fairly large rocks and began placing them into the bottom of the jar. The students watched and counted as the teacher placed one after the other into the jar. After placing about a dozen large rocks the jar was full to the brim and couldn't possibly hold any more rocks. At this point the teacher stopped and looked up at the intrigued students.

He then asked "students you can all see the rocks and the jar clearly, do you all agree that the jar is completely full?" Each student eagerly nodded affirmative and said yes it was definitely full. Large rocks up to the brim.

At this, the teacher pulled out another bag from behind the table. This bag contained small "pea gravel". To the student's astonishment the teacher began pouring the bag of pea gravel into the jar. The students were fascinated to see how much pea gravel tumbled and worked its way around the rocks and down to the bottom of the jar. Eventually the pea gravel filled the voids between the rocks and climbed its way to the top of the jar.

For added affect, the teacher shook the jar to settle the pea gravel and added a little more to again bring the pea gravel to the brim of the jar. At this point the teacher looked quite satisfied and used positive body language to further sell his actions.

The teacher again looked confidently at the students and again asked them if the jar was full. Most of the students quickly nodded yes with a few sluggish nods.

At this, the teacher grinned as he pulled another bag from behind his display table. This bag contained a fairly large quantity of regular playground sand. He at-once began pouring the sand into the top of the jar. The sand quickly disappeared down through the voids of the large rocks and pea gravel. To the bottom went the sand until it too began accumulating. Soon it was filling the voids and moving to the top. With the sand the teacher shook the jar many times to enhance the settling of the sand into every remaining crevice.

Again it was quite amazing, to the students, that so much sand could be added to an already "full" jar. When the sand was obviously running over the top of the jar the teacher stopped pouring.

Looking up at the still riveted students the teacher asked one more time if the students thought that the jar was full? This time only a gullible few seemed to slowly shake their heads yes. Most just looked on with an eye of suspicion and uncertainty. After a number of moments of awkward silence, the teacher broke into a big smile and congratulated the students on their rising level of distrust and suspicion.

The teacher said your doubts are rewarded as he pulled out a hidden jar of water from behind the table. He said, "let's look and see how much water we can pour into this "full" jar of Rocks, Gravel and Sand". He was able to pour nearly a full quart of water into the tiny spaces left in the jar before it came to the top.

Wow, the students were quite taken by this whole amazing demonstration. It was a series of paradigm shifts occurring in a matter of minutes.

The teacher looked at the students and the full jar a few times. He then asked the students what was the one main lesson they learned from this enlightening experience.

After several minutes of discussion, the class finally came to the same main conclusion:

"You can always find room to put more into your jar than you first thought you could"

The teacher smiled and agreed that that was very true and an interesting conclusion. The students could tell that the teacher's demeanor meant that the answer was not the main critical point of the experiment.

Key Conclusion:

If you don't put the big rocks into your jar first....

You will never have room to get them in later.

Unknown

MEN, Start with your big rocks first.

What is your most important "Big Rock"?

Wife, Children, Family, Friendships, Work........

17. JOY IN HORSE POOP

Eric and Evan are my favorite twin nephews. I love them and their wives (Haley & Michaela) very much. They are men of first rate integrity and ambition. I could write an entire book about the positive attitudes and actions these young men have displayed in their short lives.

Twins mean that they were obviously born the same day. They were together from conception through birth. They will always be closely connected no matter their physical distance apart. In turn, they will also continuously be connected in the hearts and minds of their family and friends. You can hardly talk about one without immediately considering the other one.

These young men have many of the same traits. They also have a vast array of totally different traits and tendencies.

It has been a constant joy to watch these boys grow and interact since their birth. Their differences are almost comical at times. "These two are twins?", we often ask ourselves. Are they even from the same family or planet for that matter? Watching Eric and Evan reminds me of an interesting story I heard years ago.

JOSH *and* JOEY

Once upon a time (I always wanted to use that line ☺) there were two small twin boys. Josh and Joey were their names. They were identical physically but their personalities were night and day different.

Josh was the life of the party. Josh never met a stranger. Josh was fascinated by everyone and everything. Josh was quick to make new friends and connect. He was a bundle of joy, excitement, and happiness. Josh had what my dad always called "a Sunny Disposition".

Joey came at life in the opposite direction. Sniveling, complaining and crying was his general state of being. Selfish and unhappy in everything and everyone. Truly what we called a "negative Nelly".

Regional Doctors were intrigued by the vast differences exhibited by these two identical twin boys. So much interest in fact that Psychologists decided to do a study on these boys. They ran many tests but one in particular went like this.

Joey (negative Nelly) was placed in a mid-sized room painted in beautiful vibrant colors. This entire room was filled with all kinds of toys. It looked like the toy store just unloaded 1 of every new "boy toy" they had in stock. Cars, trucks, Play-dough, army men, Legos, erector set, Lincoln logs, Ninja Turtle and Power Ranger figurines. Superman and Batman capes and accessories. Games and puzzles of every kind. Literally a young boy's fantasy toy land.

The parents and Doctors left Joey in this "fantasy toy-land" to play to his heart's content. After 30 minutes of unrestricted full out play the parents and Doctors returned to evaluate the state of Joey and all his new toys. To their shock, and amazement, they found Joey all curled up in the corner. He was whining and crying with no toys around him.

Quite perplexed, the Doctors quickly began evaluating the situation and asking Joey lots of questions. They asked, "Joey, why are you curled up here in the corner crying?". Joey wiped away a tear and grumpily began explaining how the race car he was playing with wasn't the right color. He wanted a blue one, not the red one they left for him to play with. Joey also said angrily that the Batman action figure was too small and didn't bend and move the way he liked. One after another Joey sniveled and complained about the toys and their not being to his liking in some fashion.

The doctors just shook their heads in disbelief and recorded the test results of Joey and the toys.

Now it was time to evaluate Josh and his reactions to his study room. Josh, was placed in a very different type of room and setting. The room was a bit smaller and painted a very drab gray color. No bright beautiful colors and shockingly no toys at all for little Josh to play with. There was only one thing in that room. It was a huge pile of horse manure. Yes, that's right. One big, nasty, smelly pile of Horse Poop.

The doctors and parents again gave little Josh the same 30 minutes of "play time" as his twin Joey had in the toy filled room.

The doctors and parents then returned to Josh and his "horse poop" room 30 minutes later. It was time to evaluate little Josh.

When they opened the door they were stunned at the sight before them. That horse poop was slung over every inch of that room. On the walls, on the ceiling it was absolutely everywhere. And little Josh. Yes, Josh was covered from head to toe with horse poop. You could just make out the whites of his eyes among all the poop smeared across his face.

He was hot, sweaty and grinning from ear to ear. He had been a busy boy.

*Josh was having tons of fun. In fact, he was so engrossed in his play that the doctors had to holler for him to stop slinging the horse poop. They had to evaluate what had just taken place here. The doctors were very much baffled at the manure everywhere. They asked Josh to explain just exactly why he was so excited and what was going on. Josh shined a huge grin and excitedly exclaimed.........**"With this much manure..... there has got to be a pony in here somewhere"!!!***

MEN,

It's time for you to grin big and start slinging some manure.

ATTITUDE – MINDSET - CHOICE

18. PLAY THE GAME

Do you find yourself on the sidelines of life? Are you just going through the motions of life? Eat, drink, work, TV, shower and off to bed. Do you catch yourself thinking or saying "Thank God it's Friday" and "Oh, God it's Monday"? Week after week is it the same aimless drudgery? A treadmill of existence that you have placed yourself on? Day after day the same old monotonous existence?

If you are just living for the weekends, then you have just trashed 5/7ths (71.4%) of your life. When I have a simple, non-thinking task I look for enhancing my life during those times. I quickly turn on an enlightening audio book, podcast or soothing music. I also look for those times as opportunities to think and plan my next productive move.

Reading 2,000 books has allowed me to meet fascinating people. I gain ages of wisdom from their lives and experience.

*Remember, **"we have to learn from other people's mistakes since we can't live long enough to make them all ourselves".***

Conversely we must learn from other people's success. That way we can rapidly and effectively build the life success we too cherish.

I have enjoyed reading books from dozens of genres. Many are deep and highly detailed. Others are simple but teach strong and valuable life lessons. One of my favorite simple lesson books is the classic "Pollyanna" by Eleanor H. Porter. It even sparked a 1960 Walt Disney hit movie under the same title. Haley Mills did a fabulous job portraying "Pollyanna" in the movie.

Pollyanna is actually a common phrase used today by people all over the world. More than 100 years after the classic book was released in 1913. The name is normally used in a demeaning way to classify someone as "simple minded", "naïve" or happy-go-lucky to a fault. An excessively cheerful or optimistic person. Actually I see it as a very sound and positive characteristic you should develop and implement daily.

NOTE: *I suppose you can live the opposite way which is described as: pessimistic, despairing, worrier, whiner, grouch, defeatist, cynic, sourpuss, complainer, downbeat, doomsayer, grump, griper, etc. (don't say you're just a realist....That's Bull).*

– Like John Maxwell says "with your attitude you see difficulty in every opportunity when you should be looking for opportunities in every difficulty".

The Story

Pollyanna is a young girl who suffers a great tragedy when she loses her mother to illness. After living alone with her poor missionary father she is hit with a second unthinkable loss. Her father is suddenly and unexpectedly stricken and dies from an illness. Pollyanna, a small young orphan girl, is then sent to live with her very wealthy aunt.

Pollyanna is quite forward and uninhibited to say what she thinks. With a very positive and friendly nature she makes connections easily. In fact, she soon has the attention and friendship of everyone she meets. She has a gift to reach out and connect with the fringe people of the town. People that are the so called "tough nuts to crack". Her sincere and friendly spirit become a contagion around town.

When she meets people of various needs and troubled situations she quickly begins to work her magic. This mysterious and simple magic soon turns a whole town on its head. When people open up about their troubles she is quick to engage them in the "Glad Game". At first, people dismiss her as using "flowers and sunshine" talk instead of properly addressing their so-called critical life issues. Before long everyone is buying-in to the sound merits of Polly's life-changing "Glad Game". Even her aunt Polly, the toughest nut of all to crack, eventually sees the light.

"The GLAD GAME"

Polly is very innocent in her approach to life and the multitude of problems each person has. She explains the game her missionary father taught her to play. Each month her father would receive a "Missionary Barrel" filled with donated items intended for home and foreign serving missionaries.

He was charged with distributing the contents of these barrels as they arrived.

Pollyanna and her father lived a very poor and simple life. Pollyanna had so much wanted a baby doll of her very own to play with. Her father said she should pray about possibly getting one in the next missionary barrel. Her disappointment was overwhelming when the next month's barrel arrived with no baby doll. In fact, the only item in the barrel was a used pair of crutches.

Her father went right to work to help his little girl fight through her profound disappointment. He sat Pollyanna down and said that it was time that he, teach her the **"Glad Game"**. *He explained that whenever sadness or disappointments come your way you have to look for something to be glad about.*

Pollyanna just couldn't see her father's point. She wanted that baby doll so very much. The only thing in the missionary barrel this month was an old rickety pair of used crutches. She looked into her father's eyes and asked how she could be glad about an old pair of crutches. Her dad rubbed his chin deep in thought.

He was trying to find the answer she needed. A big grin came across his face as he said to Pollyanna, I've got it. You can just be glad that you are healthy and you don't need the crutches. She was quite astonished by his answer at first. Then Pollyanna, slowly nodded and said, "Yes, I can sure be glad about that". She wiped her tears, gave her dad a huge hug and said "I love you".

LIFE IS NOT ABOUT WAITING FOR THE STORMS TO PASS......
.....IT'S ABOUT LEARNING TO FIND JOY IN THE RAIN.

unknown

In a final lesson about the Glad Game, her father talked about how every situation in life offers an opportunity to play. He went on to say that throughout the Bible, God put in over 800 verses telling his people to "rejoice" and "Be Glad". Pollyanna's father stated that if God told us over 800 times to "Be Glad" he must have really wanted us to do it.

MEN,
IT'S TIME TO START PLAYING THE "GLAD GAME"

Time to: **Live Your Legacy** *of Faith, Family & Freedom!*
Time to: Live a life of **PURPOSE, PASSION & PROSPERITY!**
Time to: Live Regret Free, Excuse Free and Fear Free!
Time to: Purge the Poison from Your Past!
Time to: Live the GIFT, the PRESENT......TODAY!
Time to: Mine the Relationship Riches!
Time to: Tell People ON!
Time to: Play **"the Game"!**

Time to: ***Target*** *Your Bullseye People!*

Time to: ***Sling Some POOP!***

Time to: Play Your 4th Quarter!

Time to: Discover Your ***Passion!***

Time to: ***Be the Buffalo!***

Time to: Race Your 4th and ***Final Lap!***

Time to: Be a Thinking Man!

Time to: Put in the **BIG ROCKS!**

Time to: ***Finish Your Life On Fire!***

ALL MY BEST TO YOU AND YOUR FAMILY

BLESSINGS ALWAYS – DAVE WADSWORTH

BONUS: OVERTIME OPPORTUNITY

19. IN CASE YOU MISSED IT 😊

Action Items, Key Quotes, Guide Questions and Direct Charges. *I will list dozens of these below. Implement just 1 action item and you will see* **UNBELIEVABLE** *results immediately. In case you missed it the first time through, I wanted to give you a reference table to allow quick access. I know when I read a book I try to remember the Key Points or Action Item takeaways I want to stick. I think this will be quite handy.*

DOUBLE BONUS

POEM ON ATTITUDE

Chuck Swindoll is another of my favorite people in life and I want to share his famous poem on attitude with you here.

"ATTITUDE"

By Charles Swindoll

THE LONGER I LIVE, THE MORE I REALIZE
THE IMPACT OF ATTITUDE ON LIFE.
ATTITUDE TO ME, IS MORE IMPORTANT THAN
THE PAST, THAN EDUCATION, THAN MONEY,
THAN CIRCUMSTANCES, THAN FAILURES,
THAN SUCCESS, THAN WHAT OTHER PEOPLE
THINK, OR SAY, OR DO.

IT IS MORE IMPORTANT THAN APPEARANCE,
GIFTEDNESS, OR SKILL.
IT WILL MAKE OR BREAK AN ORGANIZATION,
A SCHOOL, A HOME.

THE REMARKABLE THING IS, WE HAVE A CHOICE
EVERYDAY REGARDING THE ATTITUDE
WE WILL EMBRACE FOR THAT DAY.

("ATTITUDE" *Continued)*

WE CANNOT CHANGE OUR PAST.
WE CANNOT CHANGE THE FACT THAT PEOPLE WILL
ACT IN A CERTAIN WAY.
WE CANNOT CHANGE THE INEVITABLE.
THE ONLY THING WE CAN DO
IS PLAY ON THE ONE STRING WE HAVE,
AND THAT IS OUR ATTITUDE......

I AM CONVINCED THAT LIFE IS 10%
WHAT HAPPENS TO ME AND 90%
HOW I REACT TO IT.
AND SO IT IS WITH YOU...

About the Author

Dave W. Wadsworth *is a:*

Generous, Genuine *and* **Uniquely Diverse** *individual.*
He is an **Author, Motivational Speaker and**
a Business & Personal Coach.

Dave produces the --------
--- "Attitude 1st Radio Show" ---
which broadcasts worldwide each week.
Sarah, *his daughter, shares*
the Co-host honors on the show.

Dave also operates his own successful **Tree & Wildlife**
Management Business *that is the envy of most*
men (and many women).

Dave is a man of sincere ***Faith****, strong* ***Family*** *values and a fierce defender of* ***Freedom*** *for all people.*

Scientific testing by the Gallup Organization ranks Dave as the ***Most Positive Person*** *on the planet.*

His extensive travel and experience includes ***Key Leadership*** *positions with the* ***U.S. Government, Corporations and Non-Profit Organizations.***

THANK YOU DR. JONES

Dr. Frederick Jones is my very special friend, mentor and Book Coach. I am a #1 Amazon Best Selling Author mainly through the coaching of Dr. Jones.

Dr. Jones is a master at helping authors launch a #1 Amazon Best-selling book. His official title is "Bookologist." Dr. Jones is a successful former Attorney. He is also a former College Law Professor from Atlanta, GA. Dr. Jones is a person of impeccable character and relentless work habits. If you desire to write a book and dream of being an Amazon Best Selling Author, you must contact Dr. Jones. He has changed my life in a very significant and positive way. Contact Dr. Jones through his ***website: drfredjones.com***

ABOUT THE AUTHOR

Dave W. Wadsworth is a Generous, Genuine and Uniquely Diverse individual. He is an Author, Motivational Speaker, and Business & Personal Coach.

Dave produces the "Attitude 1st Radio Show" which broadcasts worldwide each week. Sarah, his daughter, shares the show Co-host honors. Dave also operates a successful Tree & Wildlife Management business. That business is unique, fulfilling and the envy of most men. Dave is a man of sincere Faith, strong Family values and a fierce Defender of Freedom for all people.

Scientific testing by the Gallup Organization ranks Dave as the Most Positive Person on the planet. His extensive travel and Experience includes Key Leadership positions with the U.S. Govt., Corporations and Non-Profit Organizations. Check out Dave's first book "Living in the Ditch" on Amazon. Dave just celebrated 35 years of marriage with his lovely wife Glenda. Contact Dave at his website: FINISHINGonFIRE.com

www.ingramcontent.com/pod-product-compliance
Lightning Source LLC
LaVergne TN
LVHW010551160826
845677LV00013B/3090

* 9 7 9 8 6 5 4 3 4 3 1 9 2 *